THE ULTIMATE GOOGLE SHEETS 2024 GUIDE FOR BEGINNERS

GUOVIANE MUACHILA

Copyright © 2024 Guoviane Muachila
All rights reserved.

INTRODUCTION

In today's digital world, data is one of the most valuable resources available, and how you manage and analyze it can often be the difference between success and inefficiency. Whether you're tracking expenses, maintaining project timelines, or collaborating with colleagues across the globe, you need tools that make managing and organizing data easy. Among these tools, one that stands out due to its versatility and widespread accessibility is Google Sheets.

For years, spreadsheets have been at the heart of data management, financial analysis, and personal productivity. However, where tools like Microsoft Excel have dominated for decades, Google Sheets has come into its own as a cloud-based, collaborative alternative that seamlessly integrates with the modern work environment. As more individuals and businesses transition to the cloud for their everyday operations, understanding how to use tools like Google Sheets becomes essential.

When most people think of spreadsheets, they might recall a basic grid of rows and columns, possibly filled with numbers, formulas, and the occasional colorful chart. But Google Sheets is far more than that. It's a dynamic tool capable of performing intricate calculations, automating tasks, enabling real-time collaboration, and even analyzing large datasets. At its core, it's designed to simplify how we interact with data, whether you're crunching numbers or managing a team project.

The power of Google Sheets comes from its ability to cater to everyone—from absolute beginners with little to no experience in working with spreadsheets to professionals who rely on its more advanced features to drive their projects. While many tools can seem daunting at first glance, especially for those unfamiliar with similar platforms, the beauty of Google Sheets lies in its intuitive design. It's accessible from anywhere with an internet connection, and you don't need specialized software to use it—just a Google account.

In its most basic form, a spreadsheet can be thought of as a digital ledger. You enter data, and the sheet will store, calculate, and analyze it as needed. Google Sheets simplifies the process of creating, editing, and sharing spreadsheets, making it an indispensable tool for personal use and professional settings. It offers the functionality you'd expect from any top-tier spreadsheet software, along with some powerful cloud-based features that set it apart. Whether you're using it to track your personal finances, manage work-related tasks, or even plan an event, Google Sheets can handle it all.

For those completely new to spreadsheets, getting started can feel like stepping into unfamiliar territory. Rows, columns, cells, formulas—it may all seem foreign at first. But in reality, the structure of a spreadsheet is quite simple. Imagine a blank sheet of paper divided into small, equally sized rectangles. These rectangles are called cells, and they form the basis of how a spreadsheet functions. By entering numbers, text, or formulas into these cells, you start to bring the sheet to life.

One of the most important aspects of working with spreadsheets is understanding how to organize your data efficiently. It's not just about plugging in numbers; it's about making your data work for you. For instance, let's say you're managing a budget. You'll want to organize your expenses in a way that's clear and easy to update. Google Sheets provides countless ways to structure and format your data so that it remains organized and presentable. You can categorize, label, and even color-code sections of your spreadsheet, making it easier to navigate.

Perhaps one of the standout features of Google Sheets is its ability to work with formulas and functions. If you've ever struggled with doing calculations manually, this is where Google Sheets shines. Formulas allow you to perform complex mathematical operations with just a few keystrokes. Whether you're summing up columns of data, averaging values, or finding maximum and minimum figures, formulas make it effortless. And while that might sound intimidating to a beginner, Google Sheets includes user-friendly tools that can guide you through these processes, so you don't have to be a math whiz to make the most of them.

Beyond simple calculations, Google Sheets offers powerful tools for formatting and personalizing your spreadsheets. Why does formatting matter? Imagine opening a spreadsheet filled with numbers, all in the same font, size, and style. It can be difficult to interpret at a glance. But when your data is well-formatted, it becomes easier to understand and navigate. With features like conditional formatting, you can apply specific styles to cells based on their content. For instance, you can highlight all negative numbers in red, or make cells with values over a certain threshold bold. These small adjustments can make a world of difference, helping you make sense of your data with just a glance.

As you become more comfortable with the platform, you'll begin to explore its advanced capabilities. One of the features that truly sets Google Sheets apart from traditional desktop spreadsheet applications is its collaboration tools. In a time when remote work is becoming the norm, the ability to work on the same document simultaneously with multiple people is invaluable. Whether you're part of a business team, a project group, or simply coordinating plans with friends or family, Google Sheets allows you to share your work, assign editing privileges, and track changes in real time.

You don't have to be in the same room—or even the same country—to work together on a Google Sheet. The cloud-based nature of the platform means that as long as you have an internet connection, you and your collaborators can access, edit, and comment on the same document. Changes are saved automatically, and you can even revert to previous versions if needed, making it a flexible tool for teams of all sizes. It's an approach that takes the old model of emailing spreadsheets back and forth, adds layers of convenience and efficiency, and leaves behind the confusion of version control.

Beyond collaboration, Google Sheets is packed with features that help you analyze data in ways you might not have thought possible. Whether you need to create charts, pivot tables, or analyze trends over time, the platform offers a range of data analysis tools that allow you to delve deeper into your data. It's not just about entering information—it's about drawing insights from it. Data visualization tools like charts and graphs make it easier to interpret your information and present it to others in a clear, compelling way.

And as you dive deeper into the functionality of Google Sheets, you'll discover the incredible power of automation. By using macros and scripts, you can automate repetitive tasks, saving valuable time and effort. Automating data entry, formatting, or even complex workflows that once took hours can now be handled with just a few clicks. For those unfamiliar with scripting, Google Sheets makes it accessible by offering a macro recording feature, allowing users to automate tasks without writing a single line of code.

The platform doesn't just cater to individual needs; it's also a favorite among businesses looking to streamline operations. From managing inventory to tracking sales and analyzing customer data, Google Sheets provides solutions for every stage of business growth. Its seamless integration with other Google Workspace tools, such as Google Drive, Gmail, and Google Calendar, adds another layer of functionality, making it an all-in-one platform for productivity.

Yet, what makes Google Sheets so compelling isn't just the sheer number of features—it's how accessible these features are to the everyday user. You don't need to be an expert in spreadsheets or coding to take full advantage of what Google Sheets has to offer. Its interface is designed with simplicity in mind, allowing even the most inexperienced users to navigate through the platform with ease. Step-by-step tutorials, in-app guides, and a vast online community ensure that help is always available when you need it.

The beauty of Google Sheets is that it grows with you. For those just starting, it's a simple, user-friendly tool that helps you organize your thoughts, manage small projects, and keep track of personal data. As you progress, it becomes a more powerful tool, capable of handling advanced calculations, large datasets, and complex workflows. And as you continue to use the platform, you'll discover more tips, tricks, and shortcuts that make working in Google Sheets faster and more efficient.

As you embark on this journey of mastering Google Sheets, you'll begin to appreciate how much more streamlined your daily tasks can become. You'll find new ways to optimize your time, enhance your productivity, and most importantly, make your data work for you. Whether your goal is personal growth, professional development, or simply a more organized approach to managing information, this powerful tool is here to assist at every step of the way.

So, take a deep breath and prepare to dive into the world of Google Sheets. With practice and a willingness to explore, you'll find that mastering the art of spreadsheets is not only achievable but enjoyable.

CONTENTS

INTRODUCTION 1
CONTENTS 7

Chapter 1: Introducing to Google Sheets 9
Chapter 2: Keyboard shortcuts in Google Sheets 33
Chapter 3: Getting Started with Google Sheets 41
Chapter 4: Using Basic Functions and Formulas 52
Chapter 5: Formatting and Personalizing Your Spreadsheet 63
Chapter 6: Managing and Organizing Data 73
Chapter 7: Collaboration and Sharing Features 83
Chapter 8: Advanced Data Analysis 91
Chapter 9: Automating with Macros and Scripts 100
Chapter 10: Productivity Tips and Efficiency Hacks 109

CONCLUSION 119

CHAPTER 1: INTRODUCING TO GOOGLE SHEETS

1.1 WHAT IS GOOGLE SHEETS?

Google Sheets is a powerful, web-based spreadsheet application developed by Google that allows users to create, edit, and collaborate on spreadsheets in real time. Part of the broader Google Workspace (formerly G Suite) productivity suite, Google Sheets is a widely accessible tool for managing and analyzing data in a format similar to Microsoft Excel. However, its cloud-based nature and seamless integration with other Google services, such as Google Drive, Google Docs, and Google Forms, make it an essential tool for individuals, businesses, educators, and teams working remotely or in real-time collaboration environments.

At its core, Google Sheets is designed for organizing and manipulating data. The application enables users to create tables, apply functions and formulas, and generate visual representations like graphs and charts. Whether you're managing personal finances, tracking project progress, conducting data analysis, or creating reports, Google Sheets provides the flexibility and functionality to handle a variety of tasks.

A Brief Overview of Google Sheets

Google Sheets was first introduced in 2006 as part of Google's vision to create an online alternative to desktop-based office applications. The idea was to offer a tool that allowed users to work collaboratively in real-time, breaking away from the restrictions of traditional software that required constant saving, updating, and file sharing. Since its launch, Google Sheets has undergone several iterations, each adding more features, increasing its robustness, and fine-tuning the user experience.

Today, Google Sheets can be used on any device with internet access, whether it's a desktop, laptop, tablet, or smartphone. Its functionality is not confined by hardware limitations, making it an accessible tool for anyone with a Google account. Furthermore, Google Sheets supports a wide range of file formats, allowing users to import data from Excel spreadsheets, CSV files, and more, enabling smooth transitions from other platforms.

Key Features of Google Sheets

One of the primary features of Google Sheets is its collaborative nature. Multiple users can view, edit, and comment on the same document at the same time, with changes being reflected instantly. This real-time collaboration capability is particularly useful for teams working across different locations, as it eliminates the need for back-and-forth emails and file transfers. Each user's changes are tracked, and previous versions of the spreadsheet can be restored via the Version History feature.

Another key aspect of Google Sheets is its built-in integration with Google's other services. For instance, it works seamlessly with Google Forms to collect survey data directly into a spreadsheet, and with Google Drive for storing and organizing files. Google Sheets also supports add-ons—mini-applications that extend the functionality of the spreadsheet. These add-ons can be used to automate repetitive tasks, create custom workflows, and even perform advanced data analysis.

Beyond its basic spreadsheet capabilities, Google Sheets includes an array of functions and formulas commonly found in other spreadsheet programs. These range from simple arithmetic calculations to more complex functions like VLOOKUP, pivot tables, and statistical formulas. Additionally, Google Sheets allows for the use of conditional formatting, data validation, and filters, empowering users to create dynamic and interactive reports.

Comparison to Other Spreadsheet Programs

Google Sheets shares many similarities with Microsoft Excel, one of the most widely used spreadsheet applications in the world. Both programs offer a familiar grid layout, a range of formulas, and data visualization tools. However, there are some key differences between the two.

Google Sheets stands out due to its cloud-based nature and collaboration features. While Excel has been the standard for spreadsheet software for decades, it has traditionally been a desktop application, although Microsoft has developed its own cloud-based version. Google Sheets is often favored by those who prioritize teamwork and real-time collaboration, thanks to its ability to track changes, restore earlier versions, and allow simultaneous editing by multiple users.

Another distinction is pricing. Google Sheets is free for individual users as part of Google's suite of cloud-based applications, though businesses may opt for the Google Workspace subscription, which comes with additional storage and administrative features. Microsoft Excel, on the other hand, typically requires a purchase or subscription to Microsoft 365.

One potential drawback to Google Sheets compared to Excel is the upper limit on file size and the number of rows it can handle efficiently. While Google Sheets is an excellent tool for many data tasks, extremely large datasets may function better in Excel due to its more extensive processing capabilities.

Practical Uses of Google Sheets

Google Sheets is a versatile tool that can be applied in a wide range of scenarios. Here are some common practical uses of the application:

1. **Personal Budgeting and Finance**: Google Sheets allows individuals to create simple or complex financial trackers. From tracking monthly expenses to managing investments, it offers a range of financial formulas to simplify these tasks.

2. **Project Management**: With its collaborative features, Google Sheets is often used for managing projects. Teams can track tasks, set deadlines, assign responsibilities, and monitor progress in real time.

3. **Data Collection and Analysis**: Researchers, educators, and businesses often use Google Sheets to collect, store, and analyze data. Integration with Google Forms allows for seamless data collection, which can then be analyzed directly within the spreadsheet.

4. **Reporting and Dashboards**: By utilizing Google Sheets' chart and graph tools, users can create dynamic dashboards that present data in a visually appealing and easy-to-understand format.

Why Google Sheets Matters in Today's World

As more businesses and educational institutions embrace remote and hybrid working models, tools like Google Sheets are becoming increasingly important. The ability to collaborate in real time, access documents from anywhere, and integrate with other cloud-based services makes Google Sheets a key part of modern productivity tools.

With the continuing shift toward cloud computing and the increasing complexity of data management in both personal and professional contexts, Google Sheets has proven to be an adaptable and reliable tool for users at all skill levels. Its user-friendly interface, combined with powerful features and integration options, ensures that it will remain a relevant and indispensable tool for years to come.

In conclusion, Google Sheets is more than just a spreadsheet application; it's a platform that fosters collaboration, encourages data-driven decision-making, and simplifies complex tasks. Whether you are a beginner looking to organize basic data or an advanced user performing detailed analyses, Google Sheets offers the flexibility and tools you need to work efficiently.

1.2 DEVELOPMENT HISTORY OF GOOGLE SHEETS

Google Sheets, as part of Google's comprehensive suite of cloud-based productivity tools, has become one of the most widely used spreadsheet applications in the world. The development history of Google Sheets is a story of technological innovation, cloud integration, and a growing demand for collaboration in digital workspaces. From its early beginnings to the present, Google Sheets has evolved significantly, transforming how individuals and businesses interact with data.

The Early Days: The Birth of Google Sheets

Google Sheets was first introduced in 2006 as a part of Google Docs, which later became the broader Google Drive suite (now known as Google Workspace). Initially, Google Sheets was not the powerhouse it is today. It started as a basic online tool for creating and sharing spreadsheets, designed primarily for simple tasks like tracking budgets, creating lists, and managing data sets.

Google recognized early on that the world was moving toward cloud-based computing, and the concept of traditional software was being challenged by the rise of the internet. While most spreadsheet programs at the time, such as Microsoft Excel, were primarily desktop-based, Google Sheets was designed to live entirely online. This distinction allowed it to be accessible from any device with an internet connection, a concept that was groundbreaking at the time.

The first iteration of Google Sheets was relatively basic, offering only a limited set of features when compared to Excel. However, it introduced a key feature that would eventually set it apart: real-time collaboration. While traditional spreadsheet programs allowed for the creation of complex data sets, they were largely solitary tools, meaning that only one person could work on a document at a time. Google Sheets broke this barrier by allowing multiple users to work on the same spreadsheet simultaneously, a feature that has become one of its defining characteristics.

Google's Acquisition of 2Web Technologies

One of the major developments in Google Sheets' history came with Google's acquisition of 2Web Technologies in 2005, the year before the release of Google Sheets. 2Web Technologies was known for developing XL2Web, a tool that converted Excel files into web applications. This technology became the backbone for Google's spreadsheet project, providing the necessary foundation to support cloud-based spreadsheets.

This acquisition was a strategic move by Google, which sought to leverage the technology developed by 2Web Technologies to enter the growing cloud market. The integration of XL2Web's technology allowed Google Sheets to rapidly evolve from a basic online spreadsheet tool into a more robust platform capable of handling larger data sets and more complex tasks.

Competition with Microsoft Excel

One of the key challenges for Google Sheets throughout its development history was competing with Microsoft Excel. Excel had been the industry standard for spreadsheet software for decades and was well-established in businesses, educational institutions, and households worldwide. Google Sheets entered the market as a disruptor, offering cloud-based functionality that Excel lacked at the time.

In the early years, Excel maintained its dominance due to its extensive feature set, greater processing power, and widespread familiarity. However, Google Sheets began to close the gap by focusing on features that Excel could not easily replicate in its desktop version, such as cloud-based storage, real-time collaboration, and accessibility from any device.

By focusing on innovation in cloud computing and collaboration, Google Sheets slowly gained traction, particularly among small businesses, startups, educational institutions, and remote teams. The ability to share, comment on, and work on spreadsheets simultaneously became a critical differentiator that helped Google Sheets carve out its niche in the market.

Evolution of Features: From Basic to Advanced

As Google Sheets grew in popularity, Google began to introduce more advanced features, making the tool more appealing to a broader audience. Initially, Google Sheets focused on providing the basic functionalities needed for spreadsheet creation, such as cell formatting, basic formulas, and chart creation. However, over time, more complex features were introduced, making Google Sheets a viable alternative for power users as well.

One significant milestone in the development of Google Sheets was the introduction of advanced formulas and functions, such as VLOOKUP, HLOOKUP, and pivot tables, which allowed users to analyze large data sets efficiently. The introduction of these features helped to further align Google Sheets with Excel, providing users with the tools they needed for more sophisticated data analysis.

Another key development was the addition of Google Sheets Add-ons, which allowed users to extend the functionality of the platform. These Add-ons were developed by both Google and third-party developers and included tools for data validation, workflow automation, and integration with external databases. By enabling customization through Add-ons, Google Sheets became more adaptable to specific business needs.

In addition, the inclusion of conditional formatting, data validation, and automated scripts via Google Apps Script elevated Google Sheets into the realm of more advanced data management and automation tasks. These features allowed users to create dynamic, interactive spreadsheets that could automatically adjust based on inputs, validate data for consistency, and perform automated workflows—expanding its capabilities beyond simple data entry and calculations.

The Shift to Google Workspace

In 2020, Google rebranded its G Suite collection of applications to Google Workspace, further solidifying Google Sheets' position within a larger ecosystem of cloud-based productivity tools. This change reflected Google's commitment to creating an integrated workspace for businesses, where Sheets, Docs, Slides, Drive, and other applications could work together seamlessly. The rebranding also brought an emphasis on deeper collaboration and enhanced user experiences.

With Google Workspace, Google Sheets became more than just a standalone spreadsheet tool. It became part of a connected ecosystem that allowed for smoother transitions between tasks. For example, a user could start a report in

Google Docs, use data from Google Sheets, and then present it using Google Slides—all without leaving the Google Workspace platform.

Mobile and Cross-Platform Accessibility

Another key development in Google Sheets' evolution is its accessibility across various platforms. Early on, Google Sheets was confined to desktop browsers, but the release of the Google Sheets mobile app for both iOS and Android extended its reach. With this development, users could create, edit, and collaborate on spreadsheets from their mobile devices, making it a versatile tool for users on the go.

Cross-platform accessibility is one of the key advantages of Google Sheets. As long as you have internet access, you can work on your documents from any device, whether it's a smartphone, tablet, or laptop. This made Google Sheets particularly appealing to remote teams, digital nomads, and organizations with distributed workforces.

The Future of Google Sheets

Looking ahead, Google Sheets is expected to continue evolving alongside advancements in artificial intelligence (AI) and machine learning (ML). Google has already started incorporating AI features into Google Sheets, such as "Explore," which allows users to ask questions in natural language and get answers in the form of charts or graphs. As AI and ML capabilities grow, Google Sheets is likely to become even more powerful, offering predictive analytics and more intuitive automation features.

With the rise of big data and increasing demand for remote collaboration tools, Google Sheets is well-positioned to remain a crucial tool for both individuals and organizations. Its development history demonstrates Google's ability to adapt and innovate, ensuring that Google Sheets will continue to meet the needs of users in an increasingly digital and connected world.

In summary, the development history of Google Sheets is a testament to Google's vision of cloud-based collaboration. From its humble beginnings as a basic online spreadsheet tool to its current status as a comprehensive, integrated part of Google Workspace, Google Sheets has continuously evolved to meet the demands of users seeking flexibility, collaboration, and advanced data management capabilities.

1.3 UNDERSTANDING THE PRICING MODEL

Google Sheets has grown to become one of the most popular and accessible spreadsheet tools in the world, due in large part to its cloud-based functionality and real-time collaboration features. One of the key reasons for its widespread adoption is its flexible and user-friendly pricing model, which caters to a diverse range of users, from individuals to large organizations. Google offers different pricing tiers for Google Sheets as part of its broader Google Workspace suite, allowing users to choose the plan that best fits their needs, whether for personal use, business, or education.

Free Version: Google Sheets for Individuals

For individual users, Google Sheets is available for free as part of a standard Google account. This makes it an appealing option for personal projects, students, freelancers, or anyone who requires basic spreadsheet functionality without any cost.

The free version of Google Sheets provides a comprehensive set of features that includes real-time collaboration, access to a wide range of functions and formulas, data visualization tools, and integration with other Google services like Google Drive, Google Docs, and Google Slides. Users can create, edit, and share spreadsheets, all while benefiting from Google's cloud infrastructure that ensures automatic saving and synchronization across devices.

With the free version, users are allocated 15 GB of cloud storage, which is shared across all Google services, including Google Drive, Gmail, and Google Photos. For most individual users, this amount of storage is sufficient for managing documents, spreadsheets, and other personal files. However, if a user is dealing with large amounts of data or needs more storage for projects, they may need to consider upgrading to one of Google's paid plans.

While the free version offers powerful capabilities, there are limitations to consider. The file size of Google Sheets documents is capped at 5 million cells, and some advanced features, such as premium support and administrative controls, are only available with paid plans. For most individual users, though, the free version is more than adequate for managing personal finances, small projects, or educational tasks.

Google Workspace Pricing Tiers: Business and Enterprise Plans

For businesses and organizations that require more robust features, Google Sheets is included as part of Google Workspace, Google's suite of productivity tools designed for professional environments. Google Workspace offers several pricing tiers, each with different levels of features and support, catering to a variety of business sizes and needs.

1. **Google Workspace Business Starter ($6 per user per month)**: This plan is designed for small businesses or teams that need basic collaboration tools. It includes the core Google Workspace apps, such as Google Sheets, Gmail, Google Docs, Google Slides, and Google Drive. Business Starter offers 30 GB of cloud storage per user, which is a significant upgrade from the 15 GB available in the free version. It also provides access to more advanced security features and administrative controls, as well as business-level customer support. However, it lacks some of the more advanced features found in higher-tier plans, such as enhanced data loss prevention and advanced meeting features for Google Meet.

2. **Google Workspace Business Standard ($12 per user per month)**: This plan is tailored for growing businesses that require more storage and advanced collaboration tools. In addition to the features of the Business Starter plan, Business Standard provides 2 TB of storage per user, enhanced video conferencing features with Google Meet (including recording options), and additional tools for team collaboration. This plan also introduces features like advanced reporting and auditing for administrative users, making it easier for IT departments to manage security and compliance.

3. **Google Workspace Business Plus ($18 per user per month)**: Designed for larger businesses with more complex needs, the Business Plus plan offers all the features of the Business Standard plan, but with increased storage (5 TB per user) and more advanced security and compliance features. This plan includes additional tools for data protection, such as data loss prevention, enhanced endpoint management, and access to Vault for eDiscovery and archiving. For organizations dealing with sensitive data or operating in regulated industries, the Business Plus plan provides the necessary tools for ensuring data security and regulatory compliance.

4. **Google Workspace Enterprise (custom pricing)**: For large organizations with thousands of users or those requiring enterprise-level features, Google offers the Enterprise plan. This plan provides unlimited cloud storage,

advanced security features, and dedicated customer support. It also includes tools like advanced endpoint management, AI-powered data insights, and enhanced meeting features, such as noise cancellation and in-domain live streaming for Google Meet. Enterprise users also have access to custom pricing based on their specific needs, making it the most flexible option for large organizations.

Google Workspace for Education and Nonprofits

In addition to its business-focused plans, Google offers special pricing for educational institutions and nonprofit organizations. Google Workspace for Education provides access to Google Sheets and other Workspace apps at no cost for qualifying institutions, with additional premium features available through paid tiers.

1. **Google Workspace for Education Fundamentals (free)**: This plan offers basic features for schools, including Google Sheets, Google Drive, Google Classroom, and other Google Workspace apps. It allows students and educators to collaborate seamlessly, while offering 100 TB of pooled storage and access to basic security controls.

2. **Google Workspace for Education Standard ($3 per student per year)**: This plan builds on the Fundamentals plan by adding more advanced security tools, such as advanced protection program enrollments, audit logs, and more detailed reporting features for IT administrators. It helps educational institutions protect sensitive student data and ensure compliance with regulations.

3. **Google Workspace for Education Plus ($5 per student per year)**: Designed for institutions that need the most comprehensive set of features, this plan includes all the tools from the previous tiers, along with additional collaboration and learning tools, such as advanced Google Meet features, classroom engagement tools, and personalized learning analytics. Schools also benefit from unlimited cloud storage, ensuring that students and educators have the space they need for all their files and projects.

For nonprofits, Google offers Google Workspace for Nonprofits, a program that allows qualifying organizations to access Google Sheets and other Workspace tools for free or at a significantly discounted rate. Nonprofits can use Google Sheets for various tasks, such as managing fundraising campaigns, tracking donations, organizing volunteer efforts, and analyzing data for reports.

Google One: Additional Storage Options for Individuals

For individuals who don't need the full suite of business features offered by Google Workspace but require more storage than the free 15 GB, Google offers Google One, a paid plan for increasing cloud storage. Google One plans start at $1.99 per month for 100 GB of storage and scale up to $9.99 per month for 2 TB of storage.

In addition to extra storage, Google One offers additional perks such as access to Google experts for customer support, family sharing options (up to 5 members), and discounts on Google products and services.

Conclusion: Choosing the Right Plan

Google Sheets offers a flexible pricing model that caters to a wide range of users, from individuals needing basic tools to large enterprises requiring advanced features and security. The free version is powerful enough for most personal and small-scale uses, while Google Workspace provides tailored solutions for businesses, educational institutions, and nonprofits.

Whether you're managing personal finances, running a small business, or collaborating with a global team, Google Sheets' pricing model ensures that you can access the features you need at a cost that fits your budget. By understanding the different pricing tiers and what they offer, you can select the plan that best aligns with your requirements and helps you maximize productivity.

1.4 HOW TO OPEN AND ACCESS GOOGLE SHEETS

Google Sheets is a versatile, cloud-based spreadsheet application that is easily accessible from any device with an internet connection. Whether you're using a desktop, laptop, tablet, or smartphone, accessing Google Sheets is simple and intuitive. In this section, we will walk through the steps for opening and accessing Google Sheets using different methods.

Accessing Google Sheets via a Web Browser

One of the easiest ways to access Google Sheets is through a web browser. Since Google Sheets is a cloud-based application, you do not need to install any software. Follow these steps to get started:

1. **Open a Web Browser**: Google Sheets is compatible with most web browsers, including Google Chrome, Mozilla Firefox, Microsoft Edge, and Safari. Ensure that your browser is up to date for optimal performance.

2. **Sign In to Your Google Account**: To access Google Sheets, you'll need a Google account. If you already have one (such as Gmail), sign in using your credentials. If you don't have a Google account, you can create one for free by visiting accounts.google.com.

3. **Go to Google Sheets**: After signing in, there are multiple ways to access Google Sheets:

    - Directly visit the Google Sheets website by typing sheets.google.com into your browser's address bar. This will take you to the main Google Sheets dashboard, where you can create new spreadsheets or access existing ones.

    - Alternatively, you can access Google Sheets through Google Drive by visiting drive.google.com. From here, you can click the "+ New" button on the left side of the screen and select "Google Sheets" from the dropdown menu to create a new spreadsheet.

4. **Create or Open a Spreadsheet**: Once on the Google Sheets dashboard, you can either create a new spreadsheet by clicking the blank template (labeled "Blank") or open an existing one from your Google Drive. Google Sheets automatically saves your work in real-time, so you can access your spreadsheets at any time without worrying about losing data.

Accessing Google Sheets via Mobile App

Google Sheets is also available as a mobile app for both Android and iOS devices, allowing you to work on spreadsheets while on the go. Here's how to access Google Sheets through the mobile app:

1. **Download the Google Sheets App**:

    - For Android users, open the Google Play Store, search for "Google Sheets," and download the app.

    - For iOS users, open the App Store, search for "Google Sheets," and download the app.

2. **Open the App and Sign In**: Once the app is installed, open it and sign in using your Google account credentials. The app will sync with your Google Drive, allowing you to access all your saved spreadsheets.

3. **Create or Open a Spreadsheet**: From the app's home screen, you can create a new spreadsheet by tapping the "+" icon or open existing spreadsheets by navigating through your Google Drive. Just like the web version, the mobile app saves your progress automatically.

Accessing Google Sheets Offline

While Google Sheets is primarily an online tool, you can access and work on your spreadsheets offline by enabling offline mode. This feature is useful if you anticipate working without an internet connection. To enable offline mode:

1. **Enable Offline Mode via Google Drive**:

    - Open Google Drive in your browser.

    - Click the gear icon in the upper-right corner and select "Settings."

    - In the "General" tab, check the box that says "Offline," which allows you to create, open, and edit Google Docs, Sheets, and Slides files without an internet connection.

2. **Work Offline**: Once offline mode is enabled, you can open and edit your Google Sheets files without an internet connection. Your changes will automatically sync once you're back online.

Opening and accessing Google Sheets is a straightforward process, whether you're using a web browser, mobile app, or working offline. Google's cloud infrastructure ensures that your data is always available, no matter where you are or which device you're using. With its easy accessibility and seamless integration with other Google services, Google Sheets remains a powerful tool for data management and collaboration.

1.5 DESIGN CONCEPT AND USER INTERFACE OVERVIEW

Google Sheets is designed with simplicity and ease of use in mind, making it accessible to both beginners and advanced users alike. The platform's clean, minimalist interface is built to ensure that users can focus on their data while offering a powerful set of tools that help with creating, editing, and managing spreadsheets. This section will explore the design concept of Google Sheets and provide a detailed overview of its user interface, highlighting key features that enhance productivity and collaboration.

Design Philosophy: Minimalism Meets Functionality

The overall design concept of Google Sheets aligns with Google's broader philosophy of minimalism and user-centered design. When users open Google Sheets, they are greeted with a clean, uncluttered workspace where the emphasis is placed on the content itself—the data and the cells—rather than overwhelming them with excessive menus or features. This approach allows users to focus on the task at hand, whether they are creating a simple budget or analyzing complex datasets.

Google Sheets' user interface (UI) is intuitive, meaning that even first-time users can navigate and perform essential tasks with ease. Its simplicity, however, doesn't come at the cost of functionality. Behind the clean design lies a comprehensive suite of tools that offer both basic and advanced spreadsheet functionalities, such as formulas, functions, charts, pivot tables, and collaboration features. The design is crafted to scale with the user's skill level, accommodating everything from quick data entry to more complex automation tasks using scripts and macros.

User Interface Overview: Key Elements

The user interface of Google Sheets is divided into several main components that serve different purposes: the toolbar, the menu bar, the sheet grid (where the data is entered and manipulated), and various side panels for additional options and functionality. Let's dive into each of these components in detail.

1. Sheet Grid

The sheet grid is the heart of Google Sheets and where users will spend most of their time. It consists of rows and columns that intersect to form cells, where users can input data, formulas, and functions. The rows are numbered (1, 2, 3, etc.), and the columns are labeled alphabetically (A, B, C, etc.), which makes it easy to identify specific cells using coordinates like A1, B2, or C5.

The grid layout is familiar to anyone who has worked with spreadsheet software before, making the transition to Google Sheets seamless for new users. Data in the sheet grid can be formatted, calculated, and analyzed using various tools, many of which are accessible directly from the toolbar or menu bar. The grid is infinitely scrollable, allowing users to work with datasets of virtually any size (up to the platform's limits).

2. Toolbar

The toolbar sits directly above the sheet grid and contains quick-access icons for commonly used functions. Its minimalist design ensures that users have the essential tools they need at their fingertips without being overwhelmed by too many options. Some of the most frequently used buttons on the toolbar include:

- **Undo/Redo**: These buttons allow users to quickly reverse or reapply recent actions, which is helpful when editing or experimenting with data.

- **Text Formatting**: Options for bold, italics, underlining, and changing text color are available for quick access. You can also change the font style, font size, and cell background color from here.

- **Cell Alignment**: This section allows you to adjust the horizontal and vertical alignment of text within cells, as well as merge multiple cells.

- **Insert Functions**: A button to insert functions and formulas is conveniently located in the toolbar, giving users quick access to basic arithmetic functions and more complex formulas.

- **Chart Creation**: The chart button enables users to quickly create visual representations of their data, such as bar charts, pie charts, and line graphs.

- **Data Filters**: The filter button helps users create custom filters, allowing them to focus on specific data without deleting any information.

The toolbar is context-sensitive, meaning that some icons will only appear when relevant to the current task. For example, options for merging cells will appear when multiple cells are selected, and chart editing options appear when a chart is highlighted.

3. Menu Bar

While the toolbar gives users access to essential tools, the menu bar offers more comprehensive and advanced options for working with data. The menu bar is located above the toolbar and consists of several dropdown menus:

- **File**: This menu contains options for opening, saving, printing, and exporting spreadsheets. It also includes the Version History feature, which lets users view and restore previous versions of the spreadsheet.

- **Edit**: This menu includes standard editing functions, such as cut, copy, paste, find and replace, and delete. It also provides access to undo/redo and the option to paste data as plain text.

- **View**: This menu allows users to customize their view of the spreadsheet, such as freezing rows and columns, zooming in/out, and hiding gridlines or formula bars.

- **Insert**: Users can insert various elements into their spreadsheet, including rows, columns, charts, images, links, comments, and functions. This is also where you can add notes and add-ons.

- **Format**: This menu gives users more control over the appearance of their data, including cell formatting options, number formatting, text wrapping, and conditional formatting.

- **Data**: This menu is where users can sort and filter data, create data validation rules, and work with pivot tables. It also contains the option to refresh connected data or create filters.

- **Tools**: Here, users can access the spell checker, enable notifications, use scripts and macros, or protect sheets and ranges for more secure collaboration.

- **Add-ons**: Google Sheets supports third-party add-ons, which can extend the platform's functionality. Users can access and manage these add-ons through this menu.

- **Help**: The Help menu connects users to Google's support resources, including tutorials, documentation, and community forums.

4. Right-Side Panels

Google Sheets includes several side panels on the right side of the interface, which can be opened as needed to provide additional functionality. Some of these panels include:

- **Explore Panel**: The Explore panel uses machine learning to help users analyze their data more efficiently. It allows users to ask questions in natural language, and it generates charts, pivot tables, or insights based on the data in the sheet.

- **Comments and Notes**: Users can leave comments and notes for collaborators in specific cells, which can be managed via the comment panel.

- **Add-ons Panel**: When third-party add-ons are installed, they can be accessed and controlled via the Add-ons panel.

5. Collaboration Tools

One of the standout features of Google Sheets is its collaboration capabilities. The user interface includes several features to facilitate collaboration:

- **Share Button**: Located in the top-right corner, the Share button allows users to share their spreadsheet with others. Users can set different levels of access (view, comment, or edit) and share the file via email or a link.

- **Real-Time Collaboration**: When multiple users are working on the same spreadsheet, each user's cursor is highlighted in a different color, and changes are made in real time. Users can also leave comments or start a conversation in the chat window.

- **Version History**: The Version History feature allows users to see who made changes to the spreadsheet and revert to earlier versions if needed.

Google Sheets' design concept focuses on simplicity, functionality, and collaboration. Its intuitive user interface ensures that users can quickly navigate through essential tools while having access to advanced features when needed. The layout, which balances minimalism with comprehensive functionality, makes Google Sheets suitable for everyone—from beginners creating simple lists to advanced users performing complex data analysis. Through its cloud-based nature and real-time collaboration capabilities, Google Sheets continues to be a powerful tool for both individual productivity and team-based projects.

1.6 ADOPTING THE RIGHT MINDSET FOR EFFECTIVE USE

When it comes to using Google Sheets effectively, adopting the right mindset is just as important as learning the technical skills involved. Whether you're new to spreadsheet tools or are transitioning from other software like Microsoft Excel, your approach to how you use Google Sheets can greatly impact your productivity, efficiency, and ability to leverage its features.

Google Sheets is not just a tool for managing data; it's a platform for collaboration, analysis, and problem-solving. To get the most out of it, you need to cultivate a mindset that emphasizes adaptability, curiosity, collaboration, and continuous learning. This section will explore the mental frameworks and attitudes that can help you become a more effective Google Sheets user.

1. Think Beyond the Basics: Google Sheets as a Dynamic Tool

Many users initially see Google Sheets as a simple spreadsheet program for tasks like entering data or performing basic calculations. While these are fundamental uses, Google Sheets offers much more. It's a powerful tool for data visualization, automation, project management, and collaboration.

To use Google Sheets effectively, you must adopt a mindset that looks beyond the basic functionalities. Think of it as a platform that allows you to interact with data dynamically, creating meaningful insights rather than just recording information. This shift in perspective can help you take full advantage of advanced features like pivot tables, conditional formatting, and data validation. By treating Google Sheets as a flexible, versatile tool, you'll be more inclined to explore its full range of capabilities, even those you may not have initially considered.

2. Curiosity and Exploration: Don't Be Afraid to Experiment

One of the most important mindsets for mastering Google Sheets is curiosity. Google Sheets offers a wide array of features and functions that may not be immediately apparent. To become proficient, it's essential to approach the tool with a mindset of exploration. Don't be afraid to experiment with new functions, formulas, or data manipulation techniques. For instance, if you're not familiar with pivot tables or the VLOOKUP function, take time to explore these features, as they can greatly enhance your ability to analyze data.

Remember that Google Sheets is a forgiving platform: any changes you make can be easily undone, and previous versions of your document are always accessible through the Version History feature. This means you can safely try new things without worrying about losing your work. Being open to trial and error will help you grow your understanding of the tool and uncover new ways to use it.

Additionally, Google Sheets has a robust Help section and an active online community. If you encounter a new feature or formula that you don't understand, search for tutorials or guides. Embracing a curious mindset will encourage you to continuously learn and evolve as a Google Sheets user.

3. Adaptability: Embrace Cloud-Based Collaboration

Google Sheets stands out from traditional spreadsheet software because of its cloud-based nature, which allows for real-time collaboration. To use Google Sheets effectively, you must adopt a mindset of openness to collaboration. This can be a shift for people who are used to working alone on desktop-based software like Excel, where collaboration often involves emailing files back and forth.

Google Sheets encourages a more dynamic, interactive approach to working with data. Multiple people can edit a document simultaneously, leave comments, and chat in real time. This level of collaboration allows for a more agile and responsive workflow, whether you're working with colleagues on a business report, collaborating on a research project, or coordinating a personal project like event planning.

By adopting a collaborative mindset, you open yourself up to the benefits of shared input and feedback. It encourages you to be receptive to other people's contributions and to view Google Sheets as a shared workspace where multiple perspectives can lead to better outcomes. It also fosters transparency and accountability within teams, as everyone can see who made what changes and when.

To thrive in this collaborative environment, you need to embrace the idea of teamwork and be willing to both give and receive feedback through the platform's commenting features. This will improve not only the quality of the work but also the efficiency of the process.

4. Attention to Detail: Data Accuracy and Organization Matter

One of the key challenges when using any spreadsheet software is maintaining accuracy and organization. Google Sheets is a powerful tool, but it's also only as effective as the data you input and the way you organize it. Adopting a mindset that prioritizes attention to detail is essential for avoiding errors, ensuring consistency, and making the most of the tool's features.

This mindset involves developing habits like double-checking your formulas, using consistent formats for data entries, and utilizing Google Sheets' data validation features to ensure the integrity of your data. For example, if you are working with dates, make sure that all entries are in the same format (e.g., MM/DD/YYYY or DD/MM/YYYY) to avoid confusion or errors in calculations. Similarly, when dealing with numerical data, ensure that you use the appropriate formatting for currencies, percentages, or decimal places.

Additionally, well-organized data is easier to work with and analyze. Take the time to structure your spreadsheets in a logical, coherent way, using headers, labels, and color coding when necessary to improve readability. A well-organized spreadsheet not only helps you but also makes it easier for others to collaborate and understand your data.

5. Problem-Solving Mindset: Using Google Sheets as a Tool for Analysis

Another important aspect of adopting the right mindset for using Google Sheets effectively is to approach it as a problem-solving tool. Instead of seeing Google Sheets as just a place to store data, view it as a platform for analyzing information and making decisions.

Google Sheets is equipped with powerful analytical tools that allow users to uncover trends, patterns, and insights from raw data. With functions like conditional formatting, pivot tables, and advanced formulas, users can transform complex data sets into actionable insights. When approaching a project, think about how you can leverage Google Sheets' features to break down large problems into manageable tasks, spot trends in the data, or automate repetitive tasks.

For example, if you are tracking sales figures, use conditional formatting to highlight trends or outliers in your data. If you're managing a large database, consider using pivot tables to summarize and analyze data from different perspectives. This problem-solving mindset will help you maximize the value of your data and make more informed decisions based on the insights you derive from your analysis.

6. Continuous Learning and Improvement

Google Sheets is constantly evolving, with new features and updates being introduced regularly. To stay proficient, it's important to adopt a mindset of continuous learning. Stay up-to-date with new features by exploring Google Sheets' help resources or following online forums and tutorials.

Additionally, challenge yourself to improve your efficiency and mastery of the tool. Set goals for learning new functions, automating tasks, or collaborating more effectively with others. By adopting a mindset of continuous improvement, you will not only become more proficient in Google Sheets but also more capable of adapting to new tools and technologies in the future.

Adopting the right mindset is crucial for making the most out of Google Sheets. Whether it's thinking beyond basic functionality, embracing collaboration, paying attention to detail, or approaching problems analytically, your mindset can dramatically impact how effectively you use the tool. By cultivating curiosity, adaptability, and a focus on continuous learning, you can unlock the full potential of Google Sheets and use it to enhance your productivity and data management skills.

1.7 The Future of Google Sheets and Its Evolving Features

Google Sheets has undergone significant transformation since its launch in 2006, evolving from a basic online spreadsheet tool to a powerful cloud-based platform for data management, collaboration, and analysis. As businesses and individuals increasingly rely on cloud-based services for real-time collaboration, automation, and data-driven decision-making, Google Sheets continues to adapt and expand its capabilities. Its integration with other Google Workspace apps, machine learning advancements, and innovations in data visualization are paving the way for even more robust features in the future. In this section, we'll explore the future of Google Sheets and the emerging features that are likely to shape its role in the world of data and productivity.

1. Increased Integration with AI and Machine Learning

One of the most exciting directions for the future of Google Sheets is its integration with artificial intelligence (AI) and machine learning (ML). Google has already introduced AI-powered features, such as the **Explore** tool, which allows users to ask questions in natural language and get instant data insights, visualizations, and suggested actions. The tool analyzes data patterns and offers intelligent recommendations, like which charts would best represent a data set or which formulas might be most useful for specific tasks.

As AI and machine learning continue to evolve, we can expect even more sophisticated features to be integrated into Google Sheets. Predictive analytics and forecasting could become more accurate and automated, enabling users to identify trends and make data-driven decisions without needing advanced statistical knowledge. For example, businesses could use Google Sheets to predict sales trends, optimize supply chains, or identify customer behavior patterns with minimal input.

The AI-powered autocomplete feature, **Smart Fill**, introduced in 2020, is another example of Google Sheets' evolving capabilities. This feature automatically completes data entries by detecting patterns, much like Google's Smart Compose in Gmail. As AI continues to improve, we can expect Smart Fill and other similar tools to become even more intuitive, allowing users to work more efficiently by reducing manual data entry tasks.

2. Advanced Automation and Workflow Management

Automation has become a crucial aspect of modern workflows, and Google Sheets is poised to expand its automation capabilities in the coming years. Currently, users can automate tasks using **Google Apps Script**, which allows custom scripts to perform repetitive tasks, such as importing data from external sources, sending notifications based on cell changes, or automatically formatting reports. While Apps Script is a powerful tool for those with coding knowledge, the future may hold more accessible automation features for non-programmers.

In the future, we can expect Google Sheets to introduce more user-friendly automation options, potentially through visual workflow builders or pre-configured templates for common tasks. Imagine being able to set up complex workflows—such as automatically generating reports, sending reminders, or integrating data across multiple platforms—with just a few clicks. By making automation more accessible, Google Sheets will enable users to save time and focus on higher-level tasks, even if they have little to no coding experience.

Moreover, Google Sheets' integration with **Zapier** and other automation platforms is likely to expand, allowing users to connect their spreadsheets with hundreds of other applications. This would enable smoother workflows between tools like Slack, Trello, Salesforce, and more, further streamlining business operations.

3. Enhanced Collaboration and Real-Time Communication

One of the primary advantages of Google Sheets is its collaborative nature, allowing multiple users to work on the same spreadsheet simultaneously. As remote work and distributed teams become more common, real-time collaboration tools are becoming essential for businesses of all sizes. Google Sheets has already made significant strides in this area, with real-time editing, commenting, and version history features.

Looking forward, we can expect Google to enhance these collaboration tools even further. **Live chat** or **video conferencing** integration within Google Sheets could allow team members to discuss data in real time without needing to switch to another platform. Google could also expand its collaboration features by integrating deeper with **Google Meet**, enabling users to host meetings directly from within their spreadsheets, similar to how Google Docs has been incorporating real-time collaboration during meetings.

In addition, improvements to **permissions and access control** will likely play a significant role in the future of Google Sheets. As more organizations collaborate on sensitive data, having fine-grained control over who can view, edit, or comment on specific parts of a document will become more critical. Google Sheets may introduce features that allow spreadsheet owners to grant different levels of access to different sections of the spreadsheet, ensuring that only authorized users can modify certain data.

4. Advanced Data Visualization and Analytics

As data becomes increasingly central to decision-making processes, Google Sheets will need to expand its data visualization and analytics capabilities. While Google Sheets already offers a variety of charts and graphs, we can expect these options to become more sophisticated, with the introduction of new chart types, dynamic dashboards, and enhanced customization features.

For instance, Google Sheets might offer more **interactive dashboards** that allow users to drill down into specific data points, filter results in real time, and update charts dynamically based on new data. These interactive visualizations would be particularly valuable for businesses looking to present complex data in an intuitive and easy-to-understand way.

In addition to visualizations, Google Sheets is likely to expand its integration with **BigQuery**, Google's powerful data warehouse tool. As more organizations rely on big data for strategic decision-making, the ability to seamlessly analyze and visualize large datasets within Google Sheets will become increasingly important. Expect to see new tools for connecting external data sources, querying large datasets, and analyzing trends within Google Sheets, all without needing to leave the platform.

5. Greater Support for Mobile and Offline Use

As mobile and remote work continues to grow, Google Sheets is also likely to improve its mobile experience. While the Google Sheets mobile app currently offers a range of features for on-the-go use, the desktop version remains more robust in terms of functionality. In the future, Google is likely to close this gap by enhancing the mobile interface, making it easier for users to perform advanced tasks like creating charts, running formulas, or automating workflows from their mobile devices.

Offline functionality is another area that is expected to improve. Google Sheets already supports offline access, but certain features, such as real-time collaboration, are only available when connected to the internet. Google could enhance the offline experience by allowing users to work more seamlessly without an internet connection, syncing changes instantly once a connection is reestablished. This would be particularly beneficial for users who frequently work in areas with limited connectivity or need to access data on the go.

6. Increased Customization and Personalization

As Google Sheets continues to evolve, it's likely that users will see increased customization options for their spreadsheets. Currently, Google Sheets offers a range of formatting and styling options, but future updates could provide more extensive themes, custom templates, and formatting rules tailored to specific industries or use cases.

Additionally, with the rise of AI and machine learning, Google Sheets might incorporate **personalized recommendations** for users based on their previous activities. For example, the system could suggest formulas, charts, or workflows based on your past behavior, making the platform even more intuitive and tailored to your needs.

7. Security and Compliance Improvements

As data privacy and security become more important in the digital age, Google Sheets is expected to expand its security features. Organizations dealing with sensitive data will benefit from enhanced security measures, such as advanced encryption options, stricter access controls, and more detailed audit logs. Google could also introduce features to help companies comply with various data protection regulations, such as the General Data Protection Regulation (GDPR) in Europe or the California Consumer Privacy Act (CCPA) in the U.S.

The future of Google Sheets is bright, with a focus on advancing its capabilities through AI integration, enhanced automation, advanced collaboration tools, and expanded data visualization features. As businesses and individuals continue to rely on cloud-based platforms for data management and analysis, Google Sheets is poised to evolve into an even more powerful, versatile tool. Whether you are managing a simple project or conducting complex data analysis, Google Sheets will continue to provide the tools and features needed to thrive in an increasingly data-driven world.

CHAPTER 2: KEYBOARD SHORTCUTS IN GOOGLE SHEETS

1. Open a spreadsheet in Google Sheets and go to Help > Keyboard shortcuts, or use the shortcut: Ctrl + / (Windows) or Cmd + / (Mac).

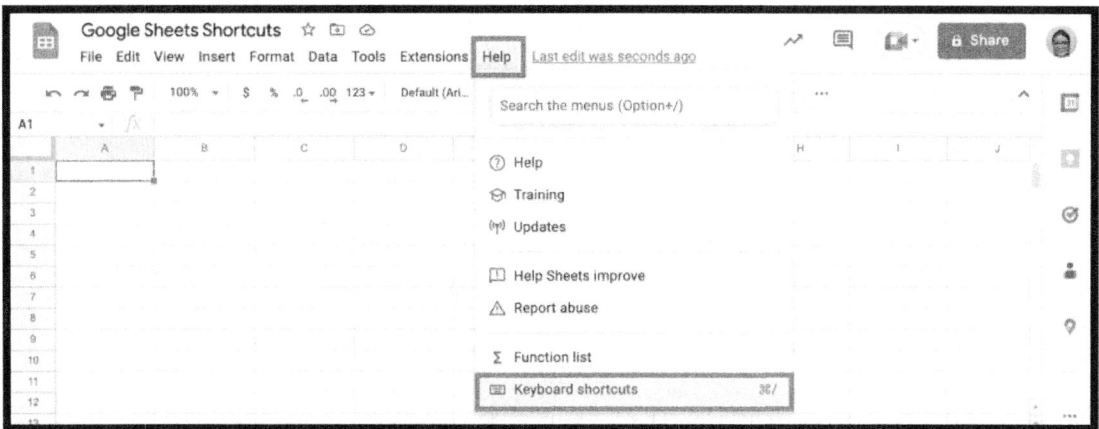

2. Click the button to "Enable compatible spreadsheet shortcuts".

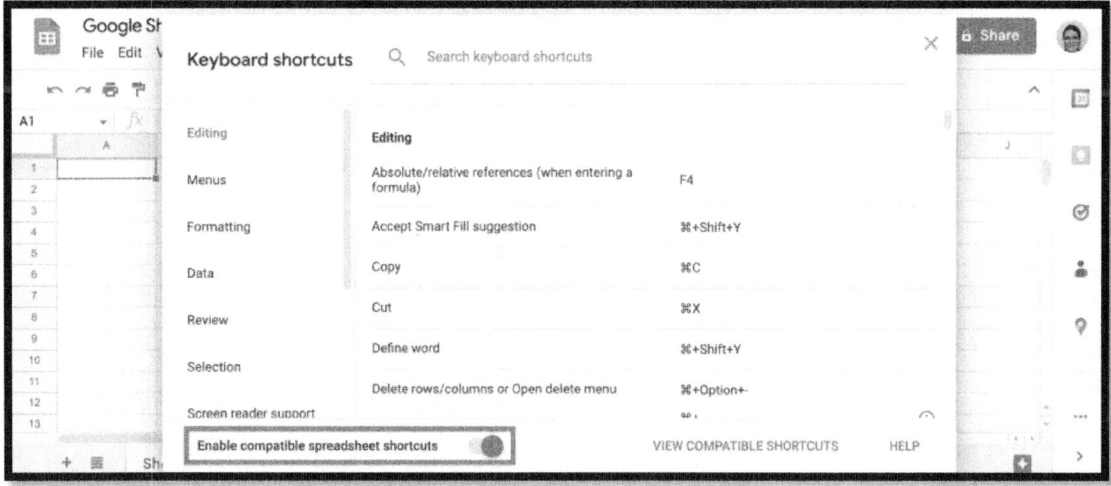

3. Click "View compatible shortcuts" to see the list.

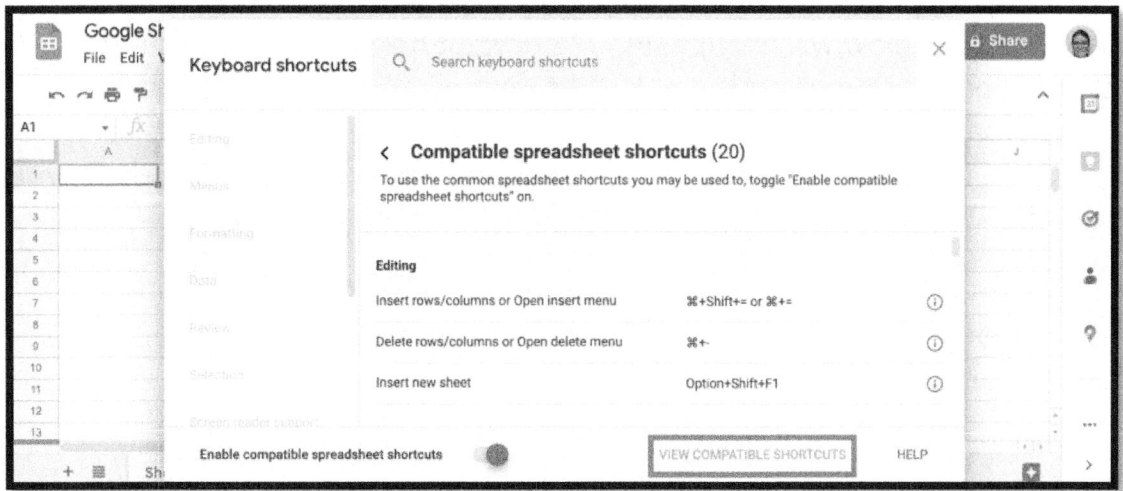

KEYBOARD SHORTCUTS FOR GOOGLE SHEETS

Below, you have a selection of must-know Google Sheets shortcuts by category for both Windows and Mac.

BASIC EDITING

The shortcuts below include common actions related to editing and selection in Google Sheets.

1. Copy

Select the cells you want and use the shortcut below to copy them.

- **Windows:** Ctrl + c
- **Mac:** Cmd + c

2. Cut

Select the cells you want to cut and use the shortcut below.

- **Windows:** Ctrl + x
- **Mac:** Cmd + x

3. Paste

Use the shortcut below to paste copied cells with their values, formatting, and formulas.

- **Windows:** Ctrl + v
- **Mac:** Cmd + v

4. Paste Values Only

Using the shortcut below will only paste the values of copied cells without formatting or formulas.

- **Windows:** Ctrl + Shift + v
- **Mac:** Cmd + Shift + v

5. Find & Replace

Use the shortcut below to open the 'Find and replace' window.

- **Windows:** Ctrl + h
- **Mac:** Cmd + Shift + h

6. Redo

Use the shortcut below to repeat your last action.

- **Windows:** Ctrl + y
- **Mac:** Cmd + y

7. Undo

Use the shortcut below to undo your last action.

- **Windows:** Ctrl + z
- **Mac:** Cmd + z

8. Select All

If you select a cell within a range, the shortcut below will select the whole range. If you select an empty cell somewhere in your spreadsheet, this shortcut will select all the cells in your spreadsheet.

- **Windows:** Ctrl + a
- **Mac:** Cmd + a

FORMAT

There are many shortcuts related to formatting, just as there are many formatting options in Google Sheets. The selection below includes some of the most common tasks related to formatting cell contents.

1. Clear Formatting - **Windows:** Ctrl + \ - **Mac:** Cmd + \	**7. Format as Decimal** - **Windows:** Ctrl + Shift + 1 - **Mac:** Ctrl + Shift + 1
2. Bold - **Windows:** Ctrl + b - **Mac:** Cmd + b	**8. Format as Time** - **Windows:** Ctrl + Shift + 2 - **Mac:** Ctrl + Shift + 2
3. Italic - **Windows:** Ctrl + i - **Mac:** Cmd + i	**9. Format as Date** - **Windows:** Ctrl + Shift + 3 - **Mac:** Ctrl + Shift + 3
4. Underline - **Windows:** Ctrl + u - **Mac:** Cmd + u	**10. Format as Currency** - **Windows:** Ctrl + Shift + 4 - **Mac:** Ctrl + Shift + 4
5. Insert Link - **Windows:** Ctrl + k - **Mac:** Cmd + k	**11. Format as Percentage** - **Windows:** Ctrl + Shift + 5 - **Mac:** Ctrl + Shift + 5
6. Insert Date & Time - **Windows:** Ctrl + Alt + Shift + ; - **Mac:** Cmd + Option + Shift + ;	

FORMULAS

There are very few shortcuts related to formulas; however, the ones included below are almost certain to be useful.

1. Show Formulas

You can show the formulas in your cells, rather than the result of the calculations, by using the shortcut below.

- **Windows:** Ctrl + ~

- **Mac:** Ctrl + `

2. Insert ARRAYFORMULA Function

When you finish typing your formula, use the shortcut below to add the ARRAYFORMULA function.

- **Windows:** Ctrl + Shift + Enter
- **Mac:** Cmd + Shift + Enter

3. Absolute/Relative References

When writing a formula, use the shortcut below to toggle between absolute and relative referencing.

- **Windows:** F4
- **Mac:** Fn + F4

NAVIGATION

There are some very useful shortcuts related to navigation that can save you a lot of clicking and scrolling through your spreadsheet.

1. Move to Beginning of Row

To move to the beginning of your current row, use the shortcut below.

- **Windows:** Home
- **Mac:** Fn + Left Arrow

2. Move to End of Row

To move to the end of your current row, use the shortcut below.

- **Windows:** End
- **Mac:** Fn + Right Arrow

3. Move to Beginning of Sheet

Use this shortcut to navigate instantly to the beginning of your spreadsheet: the cell in the top-left corner.

- **Windows:** Ctrl + Home
- **Mac:** Cmd + Fn + Left Arrow

4. Move to End of Sheet

The shortcut below allows you to navigate instantly to the end of your spreadsheet: the cell in the bottom-right corner.

- **Windows:** Ctrl + End

- **Mac:** Cmd + Fn + Right Arrow

5. Move to Previous Sheet

You can move to the previous sheet in your spreadsheet by using the shortcut below.

- **Windows:** Alt + Up Arrow
- **Mac:** Option + Up Arrow

6. Move to Next Sheet

To move to the next sheet in your spreadsheet, use the shortcut below.

- **Windows:** Alt + Down Arrow
- **Mac:** Option + Down Arrow

7. Display List of Sheets

Use the shortcut below anywhere in your spreadsheet to display the list of available sheets.

- **Windows:** Alt + Shift + k
- **Mac:** Option + Shift + k

8. Open Revision History

You can use this shortcut anywhere in your spreadsheet to open its revision history.

- **Windows:** Ctrl + Alt + Shift + h
- **Mac:** Cmd + Option + Shift + h

9. Move to Quicksum

Select the range of cells and use the shortcut to move to the quicksum button on the bottom-right corner of your spreadsheet. If you then press 'Enter', the rest of the quick calculations will be displayed.

- **Windows:** Alt + Shift + q
- **Mac:** Option + Shift + q

SELECT & EDIT ROWS & COLUMNS

1. Select Column

Click on a cell and use the shortcut below to select the entire column.

- **Windows:** Ctrl + Space
- **Mac:** Ctrl + Space

2. Select Row

Click on a cell and use the shortcut below to select the entire row.

- **Windows:** Shift + Space
- **Mac:** Shift + Space

3. Insert Column Left

Select one or more columns and use the shortcut below to insert the same number of columns to the left of your selection.

- **Windows:** Ctrl + Shift + +
- **Mac:** Cmd + Shift + –

4. Insert Row Above

Select one or more rows and use the shortcut below to insert the same number of rows above your selection.

- **Windows:** Ctrl + Shift + +
- **Mac:** Cmd + Shift + –

5. Delete Columns

Select the columns you want to delete and use the shortcut below.

- **Windows:** Ctrl + Alt + –
- **Mac:** Cmd + Option + –

6. Delete Rows

Select the rows you want to delete and use the shortcut below.

- **Windows:** Ctrl + Alt + –
- **Mac:** Cmd + Option + –

7. Group Rows or Columns

Select the rows or columns you want to group and use the shortcut below.

- **Windows:** Alt + Shift + Right Arrow
- **Mac:** Option + Shift + Right Arrow

8. Ungroup Rows or Columns

Select the rows or columns you want to ungroup and use the shortcut below.

- **Windows:** Alt + Shift + Left Arrow
- **Mac:** Option + Shift + Left Arrow

Google Sheets features useful keyboard shortcuts to save you time and effort when performing common tasks. The first of these is Ctrl + / or Cmd + /, which will open the full list of keyboard shortcuts in Google Sheets. In addition to the native shortcuts, you can also enable shortcuts that are compatible with Microsoft Excel.

You now know 39 must-know keyboard shortcuts in Google Sheets, and you have the necessary key combinations to use them on both Windows and Mac desktop computers. If you're used to using Microsoft Excel, you know you can enable compatible spreadsheet shortcuts to use Excel shortcuts in Google Sheets. However, the number of compatible shortcuts available differs according to whether you use Windows or Mac: 130+ and 20, respectively.

CHAPTER 3: GETTING STARTED WITH GOOGLE SHEETS

CREATING A GOOGLE SHEETS ACCOUNT

The most commonly used spreadsheet software that can be accessed on the web is Google Sheets. Does that imply that it Is es-sentially nothing more than Google's equivalent of Microsoft Excel? To some extent, but not entirely. If you already have experi-ence using Excel, learning how to utilize Google Sheets will be much simpler for you to accomplish. Since they are both spread-

sheet applications, a lot of their functions are similar to one another, yet, there are some significant distinctions between the two. The following are the most important takeaways:

- It was designed with collaboration in mind from the beginning, so Google Sheets makes it simple to share spreadsheets, give others permission to amend them, and work together in real-time. In spite of the fact that Excel Online now offers capabilities that are analogous to those for collaborative work, the application does not operate as smoothly as Google Sheets.
- Even while Google Sheets just increased its cell limit to 10 million, it is still nowhere near as powerful as Excel, which supports 17 billion cells per spreadsheet. Because of this, Excel is the superior tool to use when working with large amounts

of data. The good news is that the vast majority of us aren't working with data sets that are that enormous. Thus Google Sheets functions just fine.
- Excel includes more powerful formulas and data analysis features, such as built-in statistical analysis tools and numerous options for data visualization. Excel also provides a larger number of data visualization choices. Google Sheets has a "lite" version of most of these functions, but it is not even close to being as comprehensive as the full version.
To get things started, let's go over basic terms related to spreadsheets that you'll need to be familiar with in order to use Google sheets:
- A single data piece or element contained within a spreadsheet is referred to as a cell.
- A column is a series of cells that runs vertically.
- A horizontal grouping of cells that makes up a row.
- The term "range" refers to a selection of cells that can span either a row or a column or both.
- A function is an action that is already integrated into the spreadsheet program that you can use to modify data,
- calculate the values of cells, rows, columns, or ranges, and more.
- The combination of functions, cells, rows, and columns, as well as ranges, that are utilized to get a certain outcome, is referred to as a formula.
- Worksheets, often known as sheets, are the named groupings of rows and columns that comprise your spreadsheet. A single spreadsheet may have more than one sheet.
- Theentirety of the document that comprises your worksheets is referred to as a spreadsheet.

It is important that we become comfortable with Google Sheets and the features it offers before we begin the process of creating accounts, so let's do that right away. Google Sheets is a web-based program that allows users to create, edit, and collaborate on spreadsheets in real- time. Users can create, edit, and collaborate on spreadsheets using Google Sheets. Because it provides such a comprehensive set of capabili-ties-including formulae, charts, data validation, and conditional formatting, to name a few-it is an invaluable instrument for data analysis, project management, and financial planning.

You will need to have a Google account before you can start using Google Sheets. You are free to skip this step if you already have a Gmail address or if you make use of other services provided by Google, such as Google Drive or Google Docs. If you are not familiar with the Google ecosystem, however, you can create a Google account by following the instructions that are provided below.

1. Launch the web browser program of your choice and go to the address www.google.com.
2. To log in to your account, go to the top right comer of the page and click the "Sign in" button.

3. When you go to the screen where you sign in, look for the link that says "Create account" and click on that.

A Google account can be quickly and easily created by following a few simple steps, which include supplying some fundamental account information and customizing account settings. To establish an account for yourself, follow these steps:

1. Please provide the following information: your first name, your last name, the email address you would like to use, a password, and your phone number. Make sure that thee-mail address you choose is not being used by anybody else and is completely unique.
2. To finish the verification procedure, click here. It is possible that Google will require you to submit a phone number in order to validate your account and for safety reasons.
3. By checking this box, you indicate that you have read and agree to the Privacy Policy and Terms of Service. It is imperative that you go over these materials in order to acquire an understanding of how Google handles your data and protects your privacy.
4. You have the option of adding recovery information to your account, which includes a secondary email address, a security question, and other information that will assist you in regaining access to your account in the event that something goes wrong.

Adding a profile photo and customizing your account settings will bring the account setup to a successful conclusion. This step is com-pletely optional; however, doing it could make your time spent on Google more enjoyable overall.

Using Google Sheets

Easy access to Google Sheets is provided once a Google account has been established on your behalf. To get started with Google Sheets, launch it by following these steps:

1. Launch your internet browser, and go to the address www.google.com.
2. To log in to your account, go to the top right comer of the page and click the "Sign in" button.
3. Enter the email address and password associated with the newly created Google account.
4. After you have successfully logged in, navigate to the top right corner of the website and select the grid icon that is referred to as the "Google Apps" or "Google Apps Laun ch er." It looks like a little square made up of nine smaller squares similar to that.
5. There will be a menu that drops down. Simply select the icon that looks like a green spreadsheet labeled "Sheets" to get started.

Google Sheet Account

In order to set up an account on Google Sheets, please proceed as outlined in the following steps:

- Launch the web browser program of your choice and go to the address www.google.com.
- To log in to your account, go to the top right corner of the page and click the "Sign in" button. Following this link will take you to the sign- in page for Google.
- If you already have a Google account, you can sign in by using the email address and password that is associated with that account.
- Click on the "Create account" link that is located underneath the login form if you do not already have a Google account. Following this link will lead you to the website where you can create an account.
- On the page for creating an account, you must fill in the relevant fields. Please enter your first name as well as your last name in the appro-priate sections.
- Pick an email address that best suits your needs. This will be the username that you use for your Google account. If you click on the link that says "Use my current email address instead," you will begiven the option to either create a new email address with Gmail or use an ex-isting email address from another service provider.
- Make sure your account has a secure password by creating one. In order to improve the safety of your password, be sure to select a combi- nation of letters, numbers, and special characters. Check that the password is correct in the following field.
- Please supply a phone number. In order to take further precautions for your account's safety and to confirm your identity, Google may request your phone number. This step protects your account and makes it easier to retrieve it if it ever becomes necessary.
- Choose your nation or region from the list that appears below the drop-down menu.
- By ticking the checkboxes, you are indicating that you have read and agree to the Privacy Policy and Terms of Service. It is critical that you become familiar with these documents in order to gain an understanding of how Google handles your data and protects your privacy.
- You have the option of adding recovery information to your account, which includes a secondary email address, a security question, and other information that will assist you in regaining access to your account in the event that you forget your password or run into any other problems.
- If you want to, you may finish setting up your account by uploading a profile image. You have the option of either uploading a photo of yourself or selecting an avatar.
- You can personalize the settings of your account by selecting your options pertaining to language, display, and privacy.
- Click the "Next" or "Create Account" but ton once you have completed entering all of the required information and have finished configur-ing your settings so that you can go forward.

In order to maintain a high level of account safety, Google may demand extra verification from you. Follow the instructions that are dis- played on the screen, which may require you to complete a captcha or input a verification code that was provided to your phone number.

Congratulations! Congratulations, the creation of your Google Sheets account was a success. Using the credentials for your freshly formed Google account, you are now able to access Google Sheets as well as other Google services.

NAVIGATING THE GOOGLE SHEETS INTERFACE

It's time to enter into the wonderful world of spreadsheets now that you've established a Google Sheets account and are ready to get started. In this section, we will investigate the user interface of Google Sheets, walking you through its numerous components and capabilities in the process. You will be able to work fluidly with your data, develop potent formulas, and make spreadsheets that are pleasant to the eye if you have a good understanding of how to traverse the interface in an efficient manner.

The Google Sheets Home Screen

You will begreeted by the Home screen whenever you enter Google Sheets for the first time. Let's take a deeper look at some of its most important components:

- The Menu Bar is an area that can be seen at the very top of the screen, and it provides a variety of options that may be used to manage your spreadsheet It provides options that are already recognizable to users such as "File" "Edit ""View " "Insert " "Forma t " "Data " "Tools " and "Help." The most important instructions and functionalities are easily accessible via these menus.
- Toolbar The Toolbar is located directly below the Menu Bar in the top navigation. It holds a collection of icons that symbolize various tools that are used regularly. With the help of these symbols, you'll be able to complete tasks in a flash, like saving your spreadsheet, undoing or reversing changes, and formatting cells.

Spreadsheet Tabs

In the lower-left corner of the Home screen, you will see a series of tabs for the Spreadsheet. Your Google Sheets account has multiple spreadsheets, each of which is represented by a tab. You are able to work on numerous spreadsheets at the same time by selecting the tabs that correspond to the spreadsheets you wish to examine and then clicking on those tabs.

The Explore pane can be found on the right-hand side of the Home screen in your device's interface. You can better analyze and interpret your data with the assistance of this powerful feature that makes use of artificial intelligence. You can generate suggested charts, sum-maries, and insights based on your data by entering questions or queries into the search bar.

Navigation

Grid

The primary section of the user interface is referred to as the grid, and it is made up of cells that are arranged in rows and columns. Each cell in the table is an individual intersecting point that is denoted by a letter from one of the columns and a number from one of the rows (for example, Al, B2, C3). The grid is where you will enter your data and perform any necessary manipulations.

Formula Bar

Below the Menu Bar is a section known as the Formula Bar. This section displays the contents of the cell that is now selected. It is the location where you can enter new formulas, functions, or values for the cell that has been selected, as well as update existing ones. You also have the ability to view and adjust the settings for cell formatting, such as font style, size, and color.

Options for the Tools When you pick a new tool or cell type, a new set of options that are unique to that tool or cell type will show below the Toolbar. These options are referred to as the Tool Options. You have the ability to change the operation or appearance of the tool or cell that you have selected using these settings.

Freeze Rows or Columns

If you have a large spreadsheet, it can be helpful to freeze some rows or columns to keep them visible while scrolling through the data. You can do this by right-clicking on the row or column you want to freeze and selecting" Freeze Rows or Columns. "To accomplish this, first, choose the row or column that you wish to freeze, and then go to the "View" menu and select "Freeze" from the drop-down menu. Choose "Up to current row "or "Up to current column" from the available options in the dropdown menu.

Sheets Navigation

You'll find the navigation options for moving between sheets within a spreadsheet at the very bottom of the window for the spreadsheet application. You can navigate between sheets by clicking on the arrow icons, or you can create a new sheet by clicking on the addition symbol.

Zoom Controls

If you want to change the zoom level of your spreadsheet, you can do so by clicking on the % value that is placed in the bottom right corner of the window. You will see a dropdown that gives you the option to set the desired magnification level or click "Fit window" to have the view automatically adjusted to fit the window.

Working Together and Sharing

The ability to work together on a spreadsheet is one of Google Sheets' most notable advantages. Sharing and collaborating on your spread- sheet may be done in the following ways:

The button labeled "Share," which can be found in the upper-right-hand corner of the user interface, gives you the ability to invite other people to work together on your spreadsheet. When you click the button, a dialogue window will open up where you can enter the email addresses of the people whose participation you want to solicit. You have the ability to specify the access permissions that they have, such as the ability to edit, view, or comment.

Commenting and Suggesting

Collaborators have the ability to leave comments on particular cells or ranges, which can facilitate discussions and provide input. They are also able to make suggestions for improvements to the spreadsheet, but these changes will not be made to the text of the document itself. These features improve teamwork and communication inside your organization, making it easier for everyone to work together.

Setting up Your First Spreadsheet

It's time to enter into the exciting realm of making your first spreadsheet now that you have a basic understanding of the interface of Google Sheets. In this section, we will walk you through the steps necessary to create a spreadsheet from the ground up. Understanding how to efficiently format and personalize your spreadsheet is vital if you want to maximize your productivity and get closer to reaching your goals. This is true whether you are organizing data, keeping track of spending, or developing a strategy for a project.

The following instructions should be followed in order to set up your first spreadsheet:

- Visit www.google.com, sign in to your Google account, and then click the "Open" button to start using Google Sheets.
- When you arrive at the main screen for Google Sheets, select the "+ Blank" button to initiate the creation of a fresh spreadsheet that is initially blank.
- You will then be brought to a spreadsheet that is completely empty and consists of a grid with rows and columns.
- Customizing Rows, Columns, and Cells is Covered in the previous section.
- Now that you have a spreadsheet with no rows, columns, or cells, let's go over how to configure the rows, columns, and cells so that they meet your requirements:

Adjusting the Width of the Columns and the Rows

1. Simply clicking and dragging the border that separates the row numbers allows you to alter the height of a particular row.
2. Click and drag the border that is located between the column letters to make adjustments to the column's width.

Combining and Separating Cells

1. To merge cells, first, select the cells you want to merge, then right-click on the selected cells, and then select "Merge cells" from the context menu. You also have the option of selecting "Merge cells" from the "Format" menu, clicking the "Merge" drop-down arrow, and then selecting "Merge all," "Merge horizontally, "or "Merge vertically."
2. To unmerge cells, you must first select the cells that have been merged, then right-click on the selection, then pick "Unmerge cells" from the context menu. You also have the option to click on the "Format" menu, choose "Merge cells," and then select "Un merge."

Changing the Format of Cells

1. To format cells, first, pick the cells you wish to format, then go to the "Format" menu and make your selection there. In this section, you'll find a variety of formatting options, such as how to format numbers, how to style fonts, how to align text, and how to add borders.

Now that you have your spreadsheet configured the way you want it to let's go over how to add and change data.

Entering Data

To enter data into a cell, you need to click on the cell you want to work in and then begin typing. You can either use the arrow keys or the Ent er key to move to the next cell in the same column. Pressing Ent er will move you to the next cell in the column.

Copying and Pasting Data

To copy the contents of a single cell or an entire range of cells, select the data you want to copy and then press the Ctrl +C (Windows) or Command+ C (Mac) keys on your keyboard.

You can paste the data that you copied into another cell or range of cells by selecting the destination cells and then pressing the Ctrl+ V (Windows) or Command +V (Mac) keys on your keyboard.

Editing Data

You can edit the data in a cell by either selecting the cell and pressing the F2 key or by double-clicking on the cell itself. You also have the option to directly alter the contents of the cell by accessing the formula bar at the top of the spreadsheet.

In Google Sheets, the ability to make calculations and alter data is made possible through the use of powerful tools known as formulas and functions. Let's lo ok at some examples of how to use them:

Inserting Formulas

To insert a formula into a cell, first pick the cell in which you want the result to display, and then begin typing the formula followed by an equal sign (=). For instance, to add the values that are located in cells Al and Bl, you would put "=Al +Bl " into the appropriate cell.

Utilizing Their Functions:

Calculations and operations of a given kind can be carried out by functions, which are established formulas. When you want to utilize a function, type the name of the function followed by parenthesis (), and then include any arguments or cell references within the parenthe-ses themselves. You may, for instance, use the "AVERAGE" function as"=AVERAGE (A1 :A10)" to determine the average of a group of cells.

Protecting Your Spreadsheet From Loss

To save your spreadsheet, you may either go to the "File" menu and select "Save" from the drop-down menu, or you can use the keyboard shortcut Ctrl+ S (Windows) or Command+ S (Mac).

Because Google Sheets will automatically and continuously store any modifications you make, you won't have to worry about losing any of your hard work.

Changing the Name of Your Spead sheet

To give your spreadsheet a new name, locate the top-left corner of the interface and click on the name that is currently shown there. The newname must be entered into the pop-up box before selecting "OK."

Importing Data into Google Sheets

In the prior section, you were shown how to use Google Sheets to create your first spreadsheet and make any necessary adjustments to it. Now that we have your spreadsheet set up let's take it to the next level by investigating the several ways that data may be imported into Google Sheets. Through the process of importing data, you are able to bring in information from a variety of external sources, including CSV files, Excel spreadsheets, web pages, and many others. When you have mastered the skill of importing data, you will have the ability to examine and modify a wide variety of data within your spreadsheets in an efficient manner.

1. Importing Data from a Local File

Importing a file that is stored on your local computer is one of the most common ways that data may be brought into Google Sheets to be worked with. This is how you can go about doing it:

- When using Google Sheets, select "File" from the menu bar.
- Choose "Import" from the list of available options in the drop-down menu.
- Select the kind of file you want to import; for example, select "Upload" if the file is already saved on your local computer.
- You can import a file by clicking the button that says "Selecta file from your device "and then searching for the file you wish to import.
- After you have chosen the file, you may proceed to open it by clicking the "Open" button.
- Specify how you want Google Sheets to handle the imported data in the import settings dialog box. Options include whether or not to import all sheets, whether or not to convert text to numbers, and whether or not to detect headers.
- To import the chosen file into your Google Sheets spreadsheet, navigate to the "Data" tab and click on the "Import data" button.

2. Importing Data from Google Drive

Data that is already saved in Google Drive can be imported into Google Sheets with no effort on the user's part. How to do it:

- When using Google Sheets, select "File" from the menu bar.
- Choose "Import" from the list of available options in the drop-down menu.
- Select the kind of file that you wish to import, such as "Drive" for a document that is saved in your Google Drive.
- Use the drop-down menu in the dialog box to navigate to the section of your Google Drive that contains the file.
- Click the "Select" button once you have chosen the file that you wish to import, and then click the "Select" button again.
- If it is important to do so, you should customize the import. settings by doing things like picking the sheet or range to import.
- To import the chosen file into your Google Sheets spreadsheet, navigate to the "Data" tab and click on the "Import data" button.

3. Importing Information from Different Websites

You are able to import data from websites into Google Sheets, which is a feature that can be particularly helpful when gathering informa-tion in real-time or data that is often updated. The following is a guide that will show you how to import data from a website:

- When using Google Sheets, select "File" from the menu bar.
- Choose "Import" from the list of available options in the drop-down menu.
- Select the kind of file that you want to import, such as "Web Page," if you want to get the information from a URL.
- Simply type in the URL of the web page that holds the information that you wish to import.
- Adjust the settings for the import, such as by defining the range or tables that are to be imported.
- In order to import the data from the webpage into your Google Sheets spreadsheet, you will need to click on the "Import data" button.

4. Importing Data from Outs ide Sources

Importing data from a wide variety of sources is made easier with the help of Google Sheets' additional choices. Some examples of this are as follows:

- **Bringing in Information from Other Spreadsheet Programs:**

Data may be imported into Google Sheets from a variety of other spreadsheet tools, including Microsoft Excel. It is possible to upload Excel files or even link directly to Excel files that have been stored in cloud storage services such as OneDrive or Dropbox.

- **Bringing in Information from CSV or TSV Files:**

If you have data that is already formatted in CSV (Comma-Separated Values) or TSV (Tab -Separated Values), you can import it into Google Sheets by selecting the "CSV" option from the import menu and following the on-screen instructions. Just follow the on-screen instruc-tions to choose the file and choose the import settings.

- **Importing Data from Add-ons Available for Google Sheets:**

You may import data into Google Sheets from a wide variety of sources, including financial data, stock prices, social networking platforms, and more, thanks to the extensive add-on library that Google Sheets provides. Investigate the many add-ons that are available, and then download and install those that best meet your data import requirements.

CHAPTER 4: USING BASIC FUNCTIONS AND FORMULAS

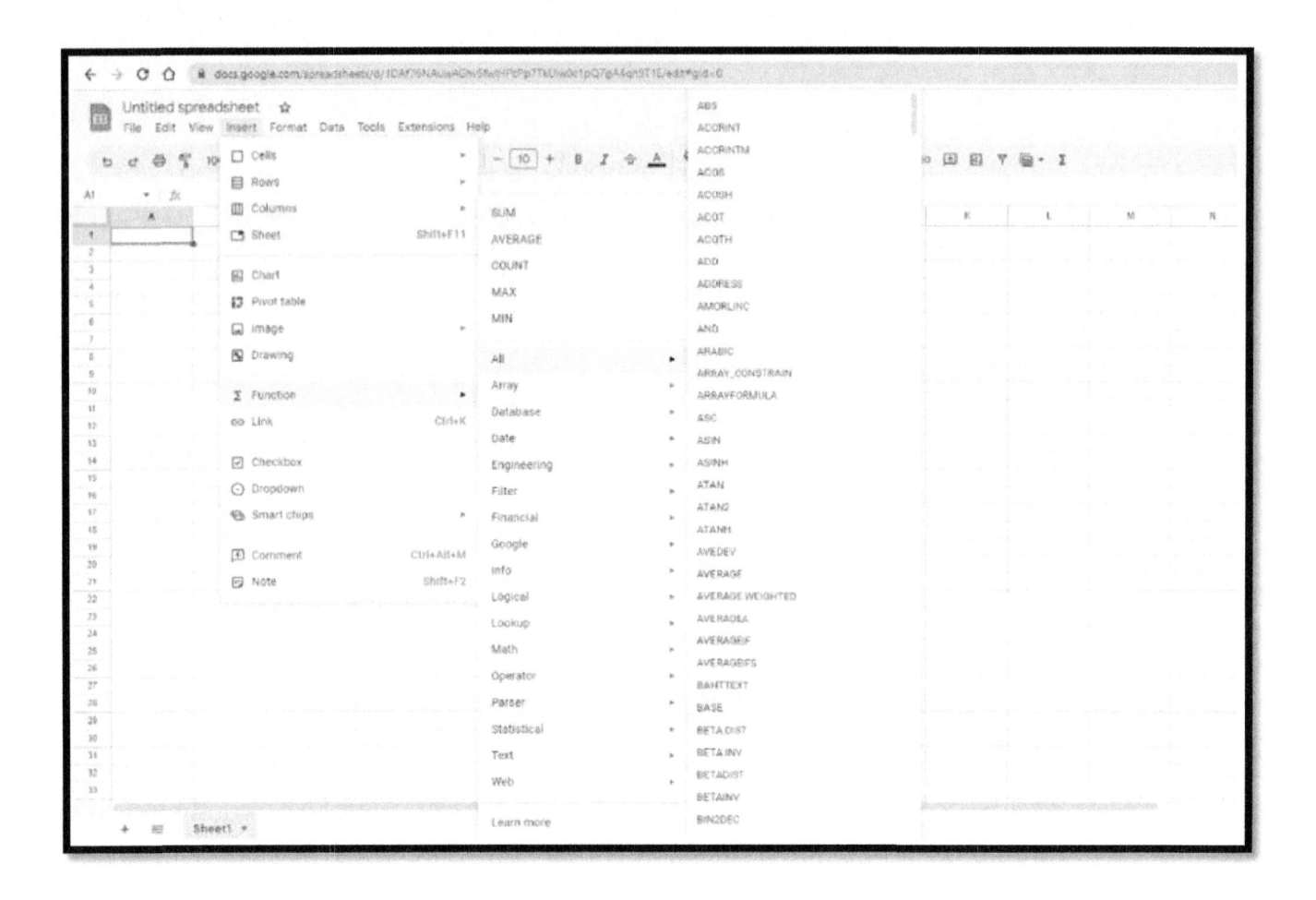

UNDERSTANDING FUNCTIONS AND FORMULAS

In the realm of spreadsheets, functions, and formulas are strong tools that allow you to do calculation s, alter data, and automate processes. These capabilities allow spreadsheets to be used for a wide variety of purposes. We will go into the fundamentals of func-tions and formulae in Google Sheets in this section, and you will be able to unleash the full power of your spreadsheet and reduce the processes involved in conducting data analysis if you have a solid understanding of how to use them efficiently.

Functions in Spreadsheets

Calculations and operations of a given kind can be carried out by functions, which are established formulas. They are made to make com- plicated computations easier to understand and to save you time. Dive in with me as we explore the realm of functions:

Structure And Syntactic Organization

The syntax and organization of functions are rather specific. The name of the function comes first, then it is followed by the parenthesis (). You should put any arguments or parameters that are required inside the parenthesis.

The following are some examples of common functions:

- SUM is an operation that calculates the total value of a group of cells. Example: =SUM(Al :Al O)
- Calculates the average value across a set of cells using the AVERAGE function. Example:
- COUNT is a function that counts the number of cells inside a range that contain numerical values. Example: =COUNT(Cl:C20)
- Returns the value that is highest in a range of cells when you use the MAX function. Example: =MAX(D1:D15)
- The MIN function returns the cell in a range of cells with the lowest value. Example: =MIN(E1:E8)

Functions That Are "Nestled" Within Others

You can exe cute more sophisticated calculations by nesting functions within each other like a bird's nest. For instance, if you want to calculate the average of a range but leave out some values, you can make use of the SUM function that is contained within the AVERAGE function.

Formulas in Spreadsheets

You are able to make calculations and change data based on your particular needs, thanks to the formulas that are included in spread- sheets. The following is information that is vital to your understanding of how to use formulas:

Formula Basics:

In order to denote that the following input is a formula and not just a standard text entry, formulas usually start with the **equal sign (=).**

In your formulations, you are free to make use of mathematical operators such as plus (**addition**), **minus (subtraction), times (multipli-cation), and divide by (division).** The order in which operations are performed can be controlled by using **parent sees.**

Cell References

In order to make reference to particular cells or ranges of cells, formulas make use of something called" cell references. "The letter that cor-responds to the column that is being referenced, followed by the row number, is what makes up a cell reference. For instance, "Al" refers to the cell that is located in column A and row 1 of the table.

In order to take advantage of absolute cell references, the $ symbol must be used before the letter of the column and/or the number of the row. This guarantees that the reference to the cell will remain the same even after the formula has been copied to other cells. Here are some examples of commonly used formulas:

- The four fundamental **arithmetic operations**-addition, subtraction, multiplication, and division-can all be accomplished with the help of formulas. For instance, the expression =Al +Bl computes the total of the values contained in cells Al and Bl.
- Calculations with **Percentages** You can compute percentages by applying the appropriate formulas. For instance, the calculation =Al • 0.1 determines 10% of the value contained in cell AL
- Conditional formulae if you want to execute calculations based on certain conditions, you can use formulae containing conditional statements to accomplish this. For instance, the formula =IF(A1 >10, "Yes", "No")checks to see if the value in cell Al is bigger than 10,andit returns "Yes" if the condition is met, but it returns "No" if the condition is not met.

Utilizing the Pre-Configured Functions and Formulas

Google Sheets has a broad selection of built-in functions and formulas that may be customized to meet a variety of requirements for data analysis. The following are some of the more prominent ones:

- **VLOOKUP** is an Excel function that looks for a value in the first column of a table and then returns another value from the same row that comes from a different column.
- The **CONCATENATE** operator joins together numerous text strings into a single string.
- **IF** is a conditional evaluation operator that can return a variety of different values depending on the circumstances.
- **DATE,** Returns either the current date or the date that was supplied.
- Calculates the length of a text string using the LEN function.

Handling Error s and Debugging

Formulas and functions are prone to erroneous execution from time to time. This is the proper way to deal with them.

Frequently Made Mis takes:

- The #DIV/0! error message appears whenever an attempt is made to divide a number by zero.
- The #VALUE! error message appears whenever a value that is being utilized in a formula is of the incorrect data type.
- The #REF! error message appears whenever a reference toa cell is either incorrect or points toa range that has since been removed.

Debugging Tools:

You may find and correct problems in your calculations with the help of the error-checking tools that Google Sheets provides. You will be able to identify the cause of the error with the assistance of these tools, which will also offer solutions to the problem.

USING ARITHMETIC OPERATORS AND MATHEMATICAL FUNCTIONS

Arithmetic Operators

- Arithmetic operators are symbols that indicate specific mathematical operations. They are used within formulas to perform calculations.
  Here are the common arithmetic operators in Google Sheets:
- Addition (+): Adds two or more values together. For example, =Al +Bl+ Cl adds the values in cells Al, Bl, and Cl.
- Subtraction (-): subtracts one value from another. For example, =Al - Bl subtracts the value in cell Bl from the value in cell Al.
- Multiplication (*): Multiplies two or more values together. For example, =Al • Bl multiplies the values in cells Al and Bl.
- Division (/): divides one value from another. For example, =Al / Bl divides the value in cell Al by the value in cell Bl.
- Exponentiation (): raises a value to the power of another value. For example, =Al Bl raises the value in cell Al to the power of the value in cell Bl.
- Modulo (%): Returns the remainder of a division operation. For example, =Al % Bl ret urns the remainder when the value in cell Al is divided by the value in cell B1.

Mathematical Functions:

Mathematical Functions Google Sheets provides a wide range of built-in mathematical functions that can be used in formulas to perform complex calculations. Let's explore some commonly used mathematical functions:

- SUM: Calculates the sum of a range of values. For example, =SUM (A1:A10) calculates the sum of the values in cells Al to AlO.
- AVERAGE: Calculates the average of a range of values. For example, =AVERAGE (B1:B5) calculates the average of the values in cells Bl to BS.
- MAX: Returns the maximum value in a range of values. For example, =MAX (C1:C10) returns the largest value in cells C1 to C10.
- MIN: Returns the minimum value in a range of values. For example, =MIN (D1:D8) returns the smallest value in cells Dl to D8.
- SQRT: Calculates the square root of a value. For example, =SQRT(El) calculates the square root of the value in cell El.
- LOG: Calculates the logarithm of a value. For example, =LOG(Fl) calculates the natural logarithm of the value in cell Fl.

Order of Operations

Order of Operations When using arithmetic operators and mathematical functions in formulas, it's important to understand the order of operations to ensure accurate calculations. The order of operations is as follows:

- Parentheses: Operations within parentheses are performed first.
- Exponentiation: Exponentiation is performed next.
- Multiplication and Division: Multiplication and division operations are performed from left to right.
- Addition and Subtraction: Addition and subtraction operations are performed from left to right.

USING MATHEMATICAL FUNCT IONS WITH CELL REFERENCES

Using Mathematical Functions with Cell References One of the powerful features of spreadsheets is the ability to use mathematical func-tions with cell references. This allows you to perform calculations dynamically based on the values in specific cells. Here's an example:

- Suppose cell Al contains the value 10, and cell Bl contains the value 5.
- In cell C1, you can enter the formula =A1 + B1 to add the values in cells Al and B1 together.
- If you later change the values in cells Al or Bl, the formula in cell C1 will automatically update to reflect the new result.

UTILIZING LOGICAL AND COMPARISON FUNCTIONS

In this section, we will explore the fundamentals of logical and comparison functions in Google Sheets. By understanding how to use these functions effectively, you'll be able to enhance your data analysis capabilities and make informed decisions based on logical conditions.

Logical Functions:

Logical functions in spreadsheets evaluate logical conditions and return true or false values. They are essential for performing conditional calculations and making logical comparisons. Let's delve into the world of logical functions:

1. IF Function

The IF function is one of the most commonly used logical functions. It allows you to perform conditional evaluations and return different

values based on a specified condition.

The syntax of the IF function is as follows: =IF (condition, value _if_true, value_if_false).

For example, =IF (A1 > 10, "Yes", "No") checks if the value in cell Al is greater than 10.If true, it returns "yes"; otherwise, it returns "no.".

2. AND Function

The AND function allows you to check if multiple conditions are true and returns a true or false value accordingly.

The syntax of the AND function is as follows: =AND (condition 1, condition 2...)

For example, =AND (A1 > 1 0, B1 > 20) checks if both the value in cell Al is greater than 10and the value in cell Bl is less than 20. It returns true if both conditions are true; otherwise, it returns false.

3. OR Function

The OR function allows you to check if at least one of the multiple conditions is true and returns a true or false value accordingly. The syntax of the OR function is as follows: =OR (condition 1, condition2.

For example, =OR (A1 > 10, B1 20) checks if either the value in cell Al is greater than 10or the value in cell Bl is less than 20.It returns true if at least one condition is true; otherwise, it returns false.

Comparison Operators

Comparison operators in spreadsheets allow you to compare values and ret urn true or false based on the comparison result. They are use-ful for filtering data and performing conditional calculations. Let's explore some common comparison operators:

- **Equal to (=):** checks if two values are equal. For example, =A1 = B1 returns true if the value in cell Al is equal to the value in cell BL
- Not equal to (>): checks if two values are not equal. For example, =A1 > B1 returns true if the value in cell Al is not equal to the value in cell Bl.
- **Greater than (>):** checks if one value is greater than another. For example, =A1 > B1 returns true if the value in cell Al is greater than the value in cell BL
- **Less than ():** checks if one value is less than another. For example, =Al Bl ret urns true if the value in cell Al is less than the value in cell Bl.
- **Greater than or equal to** (>=): checks if one value is greater than or equal to another. For example, =A1 >= B1 returns true if the value in cell Al is greater than or equal to the value in cell BL
- **Less than or equal to (=):** checks   if one value is less than or equal to another. For example, =Al = Bl returns true if the value in cell Al is less than or equal to the value in cell B1.

Combining Logical and Comparison Functions

Combining Logical and Comparison Functions, You can combine logical and comparison functions to create more complex conditions and perform advanced calculations. This allows you to build sophisticated logical expressions and automate decision-making processes. Here's an example:

1. Suppose you have a dataset with sales figures in column A, and you want to categorize the sales as "high" or "low" based on a threshold value.
2. In column B, you can use the formula =IF (A1 > 1000,"High","Low") to check if the value in cell Al is greater than 1000. If true, it catego-rizes it as "high"; otherwise, it categorizes it as "low.".

Combining logical and comparison functions in Google Sheets allows you to create more complex conditions and perform advanced cal-culations. By leveraging the power of these functions together, you can automate decision-making processes and extract valuable insights from your data. Let's explore how to combine logical and comparison functions in Google Sheets:

1. **Using Logical Functions with Comparison Operators:**
   - You can use logical functions like IF, AND, and OR in combination with comparison operators to create conditional statements.
   - For example, let's say you have a data set of sales figures in column A, and you want to categorize the sales as "high" if they are greater than 1000and "low" if they are less than or equal to 1000.
   - In cell Bl, you can use the formula: =IF (A1 > 1000, "High", "Low").
     o This formula checks if the value in cell Al is greater than 1000. If true, it returns "high"; otherwise, it returns "low.".
   - You can then copy this formula down the column to apply the same logic to the rest of the dataset.

2. **Nesting Logical Functions:**
   - You can nest logical functions inside one another to create more complex conditions.
   - For example, let's say you have a dataset of students' grades in column A, and you want to determine if a student has passed the course based on two conditions:
     o The student's average grade should be at least 70.
     o The student should not have a grade below 50.
   - In cell Bl, you can use the formula: =IF (AND(AVERAGE(Al :Cl)>= 70, MIN(Al:C1) > = 50), "Pas s", "Fail ")
     o This formula calculates the average grade using the AVERAGE function and checks if it is greater than or equal to 70. It also checks if the minimum grade using the MIN function is greater than or equal to 50.
     o If both conditions are true, it returns "Pass"; otherwise, it returns "Fail".
   - Again, you can copy this formula down the column to apply it to other students' data.

3. **Using Logical Functions with Multiple Conditions:**
   - You can use logical functions like AND and OR to evaluate multiple conditions simultaneously.
   - For example, let's say you have a dataset of products with their respective quantities in columns A and B. You want to identify the prod-ucts that have a quantity greater than 100oraquantity less than 10.

- In cell C1, you can use the formula: =IF(OR(A1 > 100, B1 10), "Yes", "No").
  - This formula uses the OR function to check if either the quantity in cell Al is greater than 100or the quantity in cell BI is less than 10.
  - If at least one of the conditions is true, It returns "yes"; otherwise, it returns "no.".
- Copy this formula down the column to apply it to other products' data.

By combining logical and comparison functions in Google Sheets, you can create dynamic and intelligent spreadsheets that automate decision-making processes and help you analyze data more effectively. These techniques allow you to extract valuable insights and make informed decisions based on specific conditions. Experiment with different combinations and explore the vast possibilities of logical and comparison functions in your spreadsheet applications.

Error Handling and Logical Functions:

When working with logical functions, it's important to consider potential errors. Here's a commonly used error-handling function:

1. **IFERROR Function:**
- The IFERROR function allows you to handle errors by specifying a value or action to take when an error occurs.
- The syntax of the IFERROR function is as follows: =IFERROR(value, value_if_error).
- For example, =IFERR OR (A1 / B1, "Error") calculates the result of dividing the value in cell Al by the value in cell BI. If an error occurs (e.g., division by zero), it returns "Error".

APPLYING TEXT FUNCTIONS FOR MANIPULATING TEXT DATA

Text functions are a set of built-in functions that can be used within a spreadsheet program to modify, format, and analyze text data. These functions are referred to as "text functions" in spreadsheets. Text strings can be combined, specific characters or substrings can be extracted, text can be replaced, text positions can be found, and text can be formatted using the capabilities provided by these functions.

Text functions are especially helpful when working with datasets that contain textual information, such as names, addresses, descrip-tions, or any other kind of text-based data. Examples of this type of information include a person's name, an address, or a description. They make it possible for you to carry out numerous operations on text data without the need for human manipulation, which saves you time and effort in the process of data analysis and processing.

Text functions such as CONCATENATE, LEN, LEFT, RIGHT, MID, SUBSTITUTE, FIND, SEARCH, UPPER, LOWER, PROPER, and TRIM are among the most frequently utilized text functions in spreadsheet applications such as Google Sheets and Microsoft Excel. Other text func-tions include these. Every function was designed to carry out a certain task and comes with its own unique syntax and usage.

You will be able to accomplish tasks such as merging text strings, extracting certain bits of text, changing or editing text, locating the posi-tion of certain letters or words inside a text string, and formatting text to fit specific criteria if you use these text functions correctly. Your capability to analyze, clean, and prepare text-based data in a manner that is more efficient and automated as a result of this is enhanced.

Text functions not only make it easier to manipulate text data but also let you derive significant insights and carry out complicated actions on textual information. Text functions simplify the process of manipulating text data. Text functions provide the required tools to do these activities within the context of a spreadsheet environment. Whether you need to clean up untidy data, extract specific informa-tion, or format text for presentation purposes, text functions can help you do all of these things.

Basic Text Functions

Basic text functions in Google Sheets enable you to perform simple operations on text data. Here are some commonly used text functions:

1. **CONCATENATE:**
   - The CONCATENATE function allows you to combine multiple text strings into a single string.
   - The syntax of the CONCATENATE function is as follows: =CONCATENATE (text 1, text2...
   - For example, =CONCATENATE"(Hello","","" and "World") combines the text strings "Hello"," "and "World" to produce the result "Hello World".
2. **LEN:**
   - The LEN function returns the length of a text string, counting the number of characters.
   - The syntax of the LEN function is as follows: =LEN (text).
   - For example, =LEN ("Hello World") returns the value 11, as there are 11 characters in the text string "Hello World".
3. **Left and right:**
   - The LEFT and RIGHT functions allow you to extract a specified number of characters from the left or right side of a text string.
   - The syntax of the LEFT function is as follows: =LEFT (text, num _chars).
   - The syntax of the RIGHT function is as follows: =RIGHT (text, num _chars).
   - For example, =LEFT ("Hello World", 5) returns the leftmost 5 characters, "Hello", while =RIGHT ("Hello World", 5) returns the rightmost 5 characters, "World".

Advanced Text Functions

Advanced text functions in Google Sheets provide more sophisticated text manipulation capabilities. Let's explore a few of these func-tions:

- **MID:**
- The MID function allows you to extract a specific number of characters from the middle of a text string.
- The syntax of the MID function is as follows: =MID (text, start, num_chars).
- For example, =MID ("Hello World",7, 5) extracts 5 characters from the text string starting from the 7th character, resulting in "World".
- **SUBSTITUTE:**
- The SUBSTITUTE function replaces specific text within a text string with new text.
- The syntax of the SUBSTITUTE function is as follows: =SUBSTITUTE (text, old_text, new_text, [occurrence]).
- The optional "occurrence" parameter allows you to specify which occurrence of the old text should be replaced. If omitted, all occurrences are replaced.
- For example, =SUBSTITUTE ("Hello, Hello World", "Hello", "Hi") replaces the first occurrence of "Hello" with "Hi", resulting in "Hi, Hello World".
- **Find and search**:
- The FIND and SEARCH functions locate a specific text within a text string and return its position.
- The syntax of the FIND function is as follows: =FIND (find_text , with in_text, [start_num]).
- The syntax of the SEARCH function is similar to FIND: =SEARCH (find_text, within_text, [start_num]).
- The difference between FIND and SEARCH is that FIND is case -sensitive, while SEARCH is case -insensitive.
- For example, =FIND ("o"," Hello World") returns 5, as the letter "o" is found at the 5th position in the text string "Hello World".

Formatting Text with Text Functions

Text functions in Google Sheets also allow you to format text databased on specific requirements. Here are a few text form at ting func-tions:

1. **UPPER, LOWER, and PROPER:**
   - The UPPER function converts text to uppercase.
   - The LOWER function converts text to lowercase.
   - The PROPER function capitalizes the first letter of each word in a text string.
   - For example, =UPPER ("hello ") returns "HELLO", =LOWER("WORLD") returns "world", and =PROPER ("hell o world ") returns "Hello World".
2. **TRIM:**
   - The TRIM function removes leading and trailing spaces from a text string.

- The syntax of the TRIM function is as follows =TRIM(text).
- For example, =TRIM("Hello World") returns "HelloWorld" by removing the leading and trailing spaces.

CHAPTER 5: FORMATTING AND PERSONALIZING YOUR SPREADSHEET

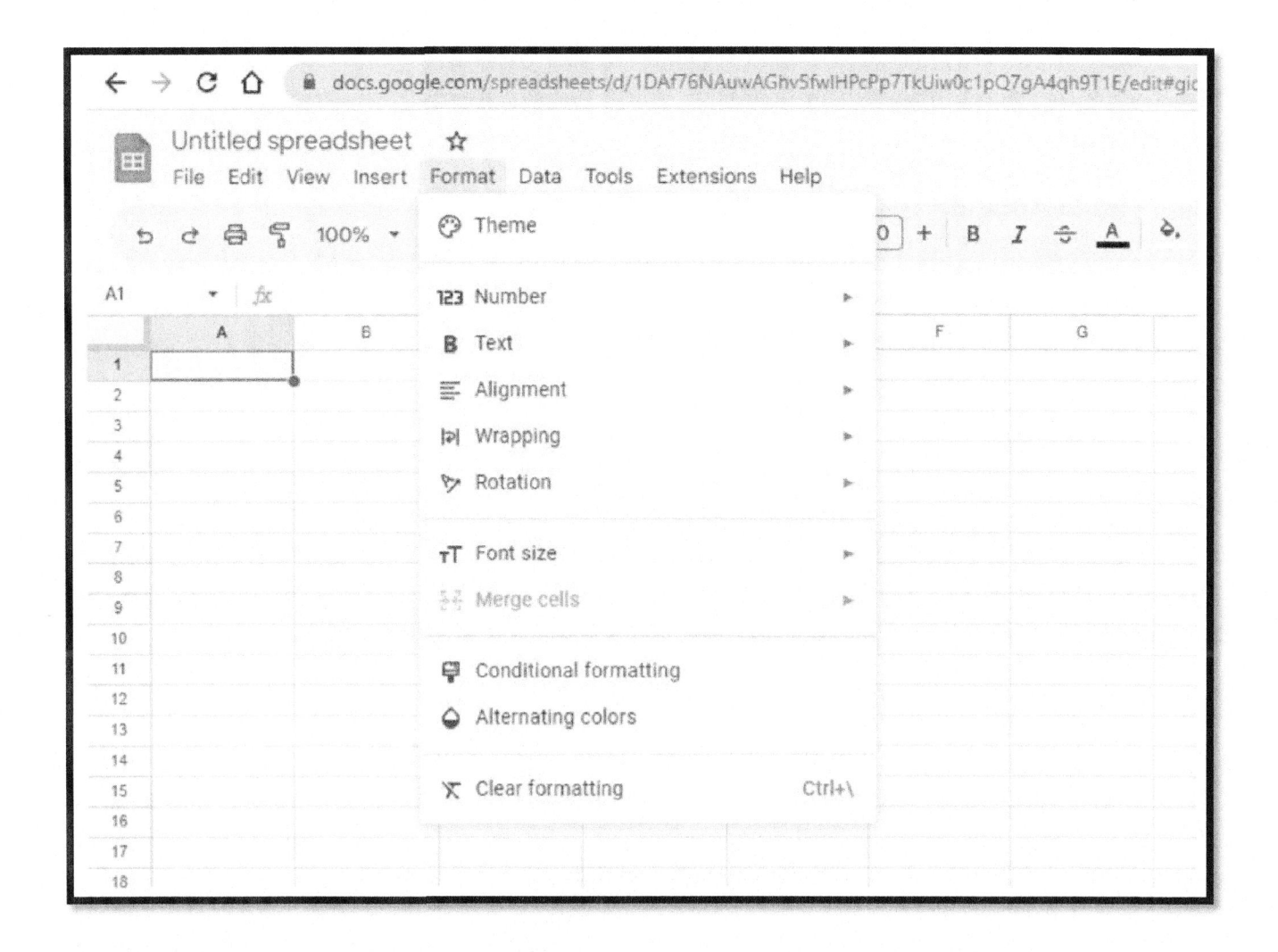

FORMATTING CELL S AND RANGES

The act of adjusting your spreadsheet's appearance, layout, and style in order to improve its readability and usability is referred to as formatting and customizing your spreadsheet. This process can also be referred to as spreadsheet formatting. It requires applying a variety of for matting options and making design decisions that result in a spreadsheet that is better structured, more aesthetically beautiful, and more successful in expressing information.

The term "formatting" refers to the process of altering the appearance of a variety of components contained within the spreadsheet. These components can include cells, rows, columns, fonts, colors, borders, and charts. By formatting these elements, you will have control over

the manner in which data is displayed, be able to emphasize key information, establish a structure that makes sense, and make the docu-ment easier to read in its entirety.

To truly personalize a spreadsheet, one must go beyond the fundamental layout of the document and instead tailor it to the user's unique requirements and preferences. It is possible that it will require picking themes, deciding on color schemes, applying uniform styles throughout the document, and altering settings to improve the display of data.

The following aims should be kept in mind when formatting and personalizing a spreadsheet:

- **Visual Appeal:**

The use of colors, fonts, and styles that are aesthetically pleasant helps to make your spreadsheet visually appealing. This is accomplished by formatting. It gives the statistics a more polished and professional appearance, which makes them more interesting to read and easier to understand.

- **Readability:**

The readability of the spreadsheet is improved by using proper formatting, which organizes the data in a way that is logical and orderly. In order to make the material legible and simple to read, it is necessary to make adjustments to the column widths and row heights, as well as to the typefaces and font sizes that are used.

- **Accentuation and Clarification:**

When you format your document, you have the ability to highlight significant data or key insights by utilizing a variety of font styles, colors, or highlighting. This helps draw attention to key information and ensures that it shines out within the spreadsheet by ensuring that it stands out from the other information.

The ability to personalize the charts and graphs contained inside the spreadsheet makes it possible to show data in a visually appealing manner, which in turn makes it simpler to recognize patterns, trends, and relationships. You will be able to successfully express the in- sights that have been gained from the data if you personalize the chart elements, such as the titles, axes, and legends.

- **Consistency:**

Customization, which applies uniform formatting styles, themes, and color schemes throughout the spreadsheet, guarantees that the spreadsheet is consistent throughout. This results in the paper having a unified and expert-like appearance.

Define Cell and Range

Any cell in your spreadsheet that you have selected and highlighted will be referred to as an "active cell" in this article. It is possible to enter data and format it in a cell that is active, but doing so will not affect the remainder of your sheet.

When there is more than one active cell in a range, such a range is referred to as a range, and ranges can either be continuous or non-continuous. A continuous range is denoted by a collection of active cells that are all located adjacent to one another. Simply clicking on an active cell and dragging the mouse to highlight cells in the surrounding area will allow you to define a continuous range.

A non-continuous range is formed when there are spaces between the active cells that make up the range. In order to establish a range that is not continuous, you must first click and drag your cursor to highlight cells while simultaneously holding down the Control key (or the Command key on a Mac).

The formatting of cells and ranges in your spreadsheet is a key step in the process of developing data presentations that are comprehen-sible, well-organized, and aesthetically pleasing. In this chapter, we will go through the numerous formatting options that are offered in Google Sheets. Th ese options provide you the ability to personalize the look and style of the cells and ranges in your spreadsheets. You will be able to efficiently format your data and make it more readable if you learn how to apply different number formats, tweak font styles, change the color of the backdrop, and add borders.

- **Number Formatting:**

Number formatting enables you to control how numerical data is displayed in your spreadsheet. Here are some key formatting options to consider:

1. Applying Decimal Places:
- Use decimal formatting to control the number of decimal places displayed in your cells.
- Select the cells or range, go to Format >Number> More Formats > Number, and specify the desired decimal places.
2. Using Currency and Percentage Formats
- Format cells to display currency symbols or percentages.
- Select the cells or range, go to Format > Number, and choose the desired currency or percentage format.
3. Date and Time For matting:
- Format cells to display dates and times in different formats.
- Select the cells or range, go to Format > Number > More Formats > More date and time formats, and select the appropriate format.

Font Styles and Alignment:

Customizing font styles and alignment improves the readability and visual appeal of your data.

1. Font Styles:

- Adjust font styles such as bold, italics, and underline to emphasize or highlight specific text.
- Use the toolbar options or go to Format > Tex t to access font formatting options.

2. Alignment:
- Align the content of cells horizontally (left, center, or right) and vertically (top, middle, or bottom).
- Select the cells or range, then go to Format > Alignment to access alignment options.

Background Colors and Borders

Formatting the background colors and borders of cells and ranges can enhance data visualization and organization.

1. Background Colors:
- Apply background colors to cells or ranges to visually distinguish and categorize the data.
- Select the cells or range, go to Format > Cell > Fill color, and choose the desired color.

2. Borders:
- Add borders to cells or ranges to create clear divisions and boundaries within your spreadsheet.
- Select the cells or range, go to Format > Borders, and choose the desired border styles.

Conditional Formatting:

Conditional formatting allows you to automatically format cells based on specific criteria:

1. Highlighting Rules:
- Apply conditional formatting to highlight cells that meet certain conditions (e.g., values greater than a specific number, duplicate values).
- Select the cells or range, go to Format > Conditional Formatting, and define the rules and formatting options.

2. Color Scales and Data Bars:
- Use color scales and data bars to visually represent data variations and trends.
- Select the cells or range, go to Format> Conditional formatting> Color scale or Data bars, and choose the desired options.

CREATING AND FORMATTING TABLES

Tables are a powerful tool for organizing and presenting data in a structured and visually appealing manner. In this section, we will ex-plore how to create and format tables in a Google Spreadsheet. Tables provide a convenient way to manage and analyze data, allowing you to sort, filter, and perform calculations easily. By understanding how to create tables, apply table styles, and utilize table features, you will be able to create professional-looking and functional data presentations.

Creating Tables

Creating tables in a Google Spreadsheet involves converting a range of data into a table format. Here are the steps to creating a table:

1. Select the data range:
- Choose the range of cells containing the data you want to convert into a table.
2. Create the table:
- Go to the Insert menu, select Table, and confirm the range of data.
- Check the "Use first row as headers" option if your data has column headers.
- Click on "Create" to convert the selected range into a table.
3. Ad just table dimensions:
- Resize the table by dragging its borders to accommodate the data.
- Add or remove rows and columns as needed by right-clicking on the table and selecting the appropriate options.

Formatting Tables

Formatting tables enhance their visual appeal and improve data presentation. Consider the following formatting options:

1. Applying Table Styles:
- Google Sheets provides a range of predefined table styles to choose from.
- Select the table and go to Format > Table Styles to apply a style that suits your preference.
2. Customizing Table Colors:
- Modify the table colors to match your document's theme or create a consistent visual identity.
- Choose Format > Table Styles > Customize to access color options for table elements such as headers, data, and borders.
3. Adjusting Column Width and Row Height:
- Resize columns and rows to accommodate the content within the table.
- Double-click on the column or row borders or manually drag them to adjust their dimensions.

Working with Table Features Tables in Google Spreadsheet offer various features that make data management and analysis more efficient:

1. Sorting Data:

Click on the arrow icons in the table headers to sort the data in ascending or descending order based on a specific column.

2. Filtering Data:

- Utilize the filter functionality to display only specific databased on the criteria you define.
- Click on the filter icon in the table headers to access filter options.

3. Adding Formulas and Calculations

- Take advantage of the table's structured layout to perform calculations easily.
- Use formulas like SUM, AVERAGE, and COUNT to perform calculations on specific columns or rows.

4. Total Row:
- Enable the total row option to display a row at the bottom of the table that summarizes the data in selected columns.
- Right-click on the table, select "Table Options," and check the "Total Row" box.

INSERTING AND FORMATTING CHARTS AND GRAPHS

Charts and graphs are powerful visual tools that allow you to present data in a visually engaging and easily understandable format. In this section, we will explore how to insert and format charts and graphs in a Google Spreadsheet. By understanding the different types of charts available, customizing their appearance, and effectively presenting data, you can create compelling visual representations that effectively communicate insights and trends.

Inserting Charts and Graphs:

Inserting charts and graphs into a Google Spreadsheet is a straightforward process. Here's how you can do it:

1. Select Data Range:
- Choose the range of data you want to visualize in your chart or graph.
2. Insert Chart:
- Go to the Insert menu and select "Chart."
- Choose the chart type that best suits your data, such as column, bar, line, pie, or scatter.
- Confirm the data range and select the options for series, headers, and labels.
3. Customize Chart:
- After inserting the chart, you can further customize it by adjusting its size, position, and title.
- Use the chart editor to modify the chart elements, such as axes, legends, and data labels.

For matting Chart s and Graphs

Formatting charts and graphs enhance their visual appeal and improve data comprehension. Consider the following formatting options:

1. Chart Styles:
- Google Sheets offers a variety of predefined chart styles that you can apply with a single click.
- Use the chart editor to access different style options and choose the one that best suits your data and presentation.
2. Color and font formatting:
- Modify the color scheme and font styles to match your document's theme or create a visually consistent design.
- Use the chart editor to adjust colors, fonts, and font sizes for chart elements such as titles, labels, and datapoints.
3. Dat a Series Form at ting:
- Differentiate data series within your chart by using different colors, markers, or line styles.
- Select the data series in the chart editor and apply formatting options specific to that series.

Chart Options and Features Google Spreadsheet offers various options and features to enhance your charts and provide a more in -depth analysis.

1. Data Labels and Annotations:
- Add data labels to display specific values on the chart, making it easier to interpret.
- Use annotations to provide additional context or explanations for specific data points or trends.
2. Trendlines:
- Include trendlines in your charts to visualize and analyze trends in your data.
- Trendlines can be helpful for identifying patterns, forecasting, and making predictions.
3. Chart Interaction:
- Enable interactive features like datapoint highlighting, tooltips, and data filtering to enhance the user experience and data exploration.
- Use the chart editor to customize these interactive features based on your specific requirements.
4. Chart Collaboration and Publishing:
- Share your charts with others and collaborate in real-time by granting access or embedding charts in other documents or websites.
- Publish your charts as images or interactive web-based charts to reach a broader audience.

USING CONDITIONAL FORMATTING FOR DATA VISUALIZATION

The use of conditional formatting might assist in drawing attention to recurring themes and trends present in your data. For example, the following monthly temperature data has cell colors that are related to the respective cell values. To make use of it, you must first develop rules that define the format of cells based on their values.

The use of conditional formatting in data visualization provides a number of benefits that improve the readability of the data and its inter-pretation. Here are several significant advantages:

- Conditional format ting enables you to graphically highlight patterns and trends present in your data, and it gives you the ability to do it in a variety of ways. You will be able to easily recognize high or low values, outliers, or major changes in your data if you apply different colors, data bars, or icon sets based on certain situations. Because of the emphasis placed on visuals, it is now much simpler to discover patterns, establish connections, and derive insights from the data.
- Readability of the Data is Improved Conditional formatting, which adds visual clues to the cells, and helps to improve the readabil-ity of the data. Users are able to immediately grasp the relevance of data points based on the formatting that has been applied, as opposed to spending time looking through rows and columns of raw information. The use of color scales, data bars, or icon sets offers a clear depiction of data changes, making it easier to analyze and compare values within the dataset. This makes the usage of these visualization techniques highly recommended.
- Simplifying Data Analysis Conditional formatting helps to simplify data analysis by calling attention to particular datapoints that are in compliance with a set of predetermined criteria. You will be able to concentrate on studying the subsets of the data that require further investigation if you first visually highlight the cells in the document that conforms to the criteria you have established in advance. This speeds up the analysis process and makes it easier to spot crucial data points, outliers, and abnor-malities in the data.
- Conditional formatting's visual impact provides an aid to decision-making processes, which is one of the ways in which it facilitates decision-making. Decision-makers are able to swiftly comprehend the most important take aways and make choices based on accurate information if the data is presented in a fashion that is aesthetically appealing. Conditional formatting makes it easier to interpret complex data and make appropriate decisions depending on the visual cues, which can be useful for recognizing sales patterns, monitoring the development of projects, and tracking performance measures, among other things.

By applying color scales, data bars, icon sets, and custom formulas, you can create impactful visual representations that make data inter-pretation and analysis more accessible.

Applying Color Scales Color scales are an effective way to visualize data variations and patterns. Here's how you can use color scales for conditional formatting:

1. **Select the data range:**
- Choose the range of cells you want to apply the color scale to.
2. **Apply Color Scale:**
- Go to Format > Conditional Formatting > Color Scale.

- Choose the color scale type (e.g., green to red, blue to white) that best represents your data.
- Set the minimum and maximum values, or use the "Automatic" option to automatically determine the scale.

3. **Customize the Color Scale:**
- Adjust the color scale's settings, such as the number of color steps, the midpoint value, and the color rules.

Using Data Bars Data bars provide a visual representation of data values within a range. Follow these steps to use data bars for conditional formatting:

1. **Select the data range:**
- Choose the range of cells you want to apply the data bars to.
2. **Apply Data Bars:**
- Go to Format > Conditional Formatting > Data Bars.
- Choose the data bar type (e.g., solid or gradient) and orientation (horizontal or vertical).
- Set the minimum and maximum values or use the "Automatic" option.
3. **Customize Data Bars:**
- Adjust the data bars' settings, such as the color, bar width, and
- Bar direction to suit your preferences.

Utilizing Icon Sets Icon sets allow you to display symbols or icons based on specific conditions. Here's how you can use icon sets for condi-tional formatting:

1. **Select the data range:**
- Choose the range of cells you want to apply the icon sets.
2. **Apply Icon Sets:**
- Go to Format > Conditional Formatting > Icon Sets.
- Choose the icon set style (e.g., arrows, shapes) that best represents your data.
- Set the rules for each icon, specifying the conditions that trigger their display.
3. **Customize Icon Sets:**
- Adjust the icon set's settings, such as the icon style, size, and thresholds for each icon.
- Creating Custom Formulas: Custom formulas provide advanced conditional formatting options based on your specific requirements. Fol-low these steps to create custom formulas:
1. **Select the data range:**
- Choose the range of cells you want to apply the custom formula to.
2. **Apply Custom Formula:**
- Go to Format > Conditional Formatting > Custom Formula.
- Enter the formula that evaluates to either true or false based on the condition you want to apply.
- Make sure the formula references the active cell using the format A1.

3. Customize Formatting:
- Specify the formatting options, such as font color, background color, or cell borders, for the cells that meet the custom formula condition.

CHAPTER 6: MANAGING AND ORGANIZING DATA

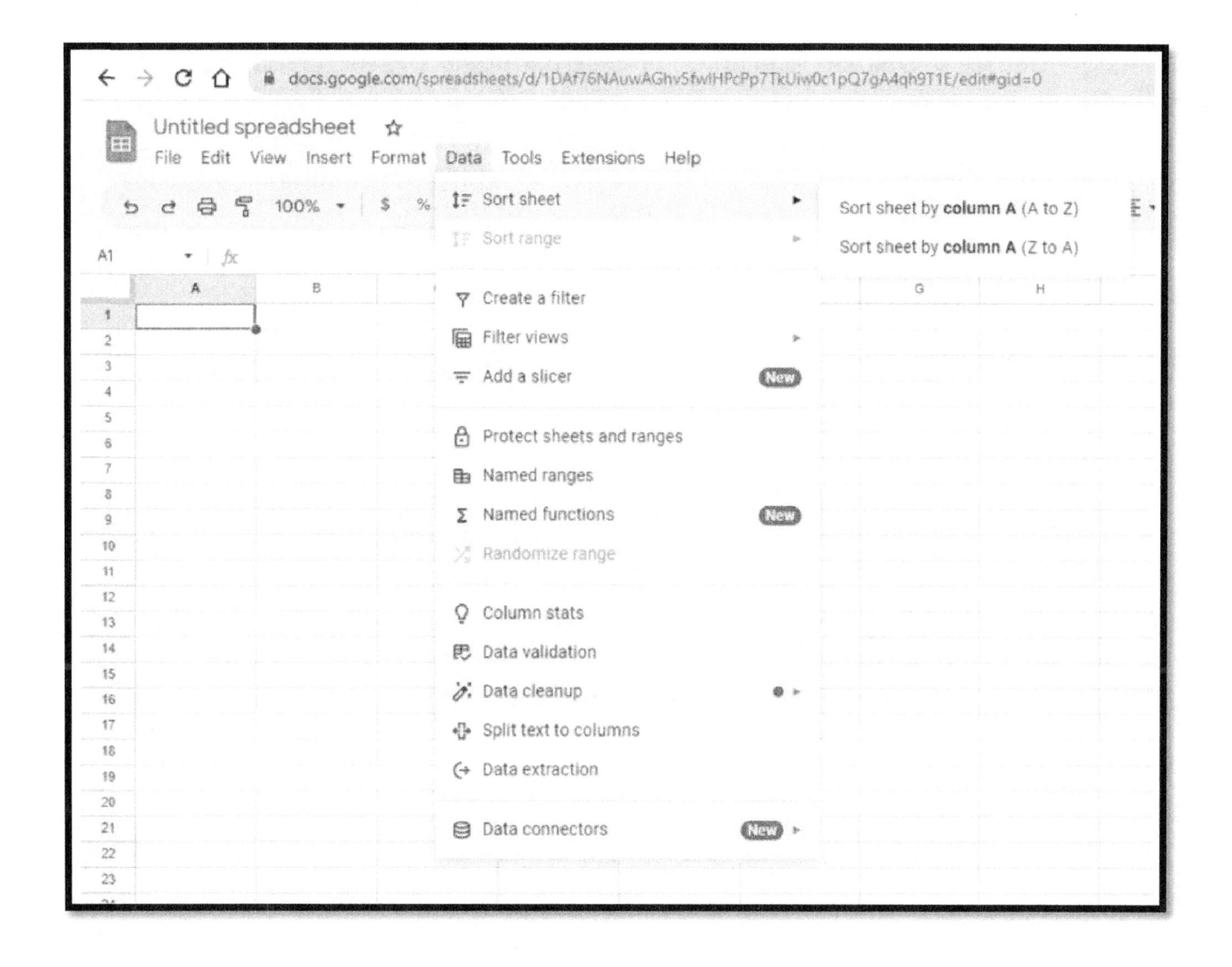

SORTING DATA IN GOOGLE SHEETS

When talking about organizing and manipulating data within a spreadsheet, terms such as sorting, filtering, and managing data in Google Spreadsheet relate to the several methods and tools that are accessible. In order to properly manage and analyze your data, these functions make it possible for you to do a variety of actions, such as arranging data in the appro-priate order, extracting specific subsets of data based on criteria, and so on. Let's take a closer look at each of these facets in greater depth:

Data Sorting

The process of data sorting involves rearranging the rows or columns of a spreadsheet depending on certain criteria, such as alphabetical order, numerical order, or custom sorting rules. You can sort data in Google Spreadsheet by ascending or descending order, sort by multi-ple columns, and even construct your own custom sort orders with the help of the tool called "sorting." The data can be sorted to assist in organizing the information and make it easier to find certain data points.

Filtering Data

Creating a Subset of Data depending on precise parameters Filtering the data gives you the ability to display only the precise rows that fulfill certain criteria, thereby allowing you to create a subset of data depending on the parameters that you provide. You can hide irrele-vant data with filtering, hone in on specific categories or numbers, or isolate data that satisfies specified criteria if you use this technique. Google Spreadsheet provides users with a number of different filtering choices, such as basic filters, advanced filters with custom condi-tions, and filter views for more complicated filtering needs.

Data Management

Data management entails conducting a variety of procedures in order to handle and manipulate the data included inside the spreadsheet. This comprises operations such as entering or deleting rows and columns, copying and pasting data, moving data within the spreadsheet, and conducting calculations or data transformations using formulae and functions. Other tasks that fall under this category include mov-ing data inside the spreadsheet and copying and pasting data. In addition, managing data requires doing actions such as renaming sheets, merging cells, securing data with permissions, and sharing the spreadsheet with other people who are working together.

Data Validation

Data validation is a feature that helps assure the integrity of data by providing certain criteria or rules for the entering of data in cells. Data validation is also known as data checking. It gives you the ability to restrict or validate the input data by defining acceptable ranges, data types, and custom validation rules. Within the spreadsheet, data validation can assist in the prevention of errors, the maintenance of con-sistency, and the enforcement of data quality standards.

Tools for Data Analysis Google Spreadsheet has a number of data analysis tools that may be used to make computations, summarize data, and obtain insights. These tools can be found in the built-in menu. These tools include functions for calculating mathematical and statis- tical values, pivot tables for summarizing and analyzing data, and an Explore feature that provides automatic insights and visualization options based on the data range that was selected.

Sorting data is an essential task in data management and analysis. Google Sheets provides powerful sorting capabilities that allow you to organize your data in a specific order based on various criteria. In this chapter, we will explore the different methods and techniques for sorting data in Google Sheet s. Whether you need to sort alphabetically, numerically, or based on custom rules, mastering the art of sorting data will greatly enhance your data organization and analysis skills.

- **Sorting a Single Column:**

Sorting a single column is a fundamental sorting technique that allows you to arrange data in either ascending or descending order. Here's how you can sort a single column in Google Sheets:

1. Select the column:
- Click on the column letter to select the entire column, or click and drag to select specific cells within the column.
2. Sort the column:
- Go to Data > Sort the sheet by column.
- Choose the desired sorting order: A-Z or Z-A for text data, or Smallest to Largest or Largest to Smallest for numerical data.
- Click "Sort" to apply the sorting to the selected column.
3. Customizing the sorting:
- You can customize the sorting options by clicking on the "Sort range" dialog box. Here, you can choose to sort by values, by the color of cells, or by the cell's format.
- **Sorting Multiple Columns:**

Sorting multiple columns is useful when you need to sort data based on multiple criteria. For example, you might want to sort a list of sales data first by date and then by sales amount. Here's how to sort multiple columns in Google Sheets:

1. Select the data range:
- Click and drag to select the range of cells containing the data you want to sort.
2. Sort the Data Range:
- Go to Data > Sort Range.
- Specify the sorting criteria by selecting the column to sort by and the desired sorting order.
- Add additional sorting criteria by clicking on the "Add another sort column" button.
- Set the sorting order for each column, and click "Sort" to apply the sorting to the selected data range.
3. Customizing the sorting:
- You can further customize the sorting options by clicking on the "Sort range" dialog box. Here, you can choose to sort by values, by the color of cells, or by the cell's format for each column.
- **Sorting by Custom Rules:**

Sorting by custom rules allows you to define your own sorting order based on specific criteria. This is particularly useful when you have non-alphanumeric data or want to prioritize certain values over others. Here's how to sort by custom rules in Google Sheets:

1. Create a custom sorting order:
    - Create a new column next to your data and assign a numerical value or a keyword to each unique value based on your desired sorting order.

2. Select the data range:
   - Click and drag to select the range of cells containing both the original data and the custom sorting order.
3. Sort by the custom rule:
   - Go to Dat a > Sort Range.
   - Select the column with the custom sorting order as the primary sort column.
   - Choose the desired sorting order.
   - Click "Sort" to apply the sorting to the selected data range.

Sorting Options and Tips

- **Sorting Options:**

Google Sheets offers additional sorting options, such assorting by color or sorting by condition. These options allow you to sort databased on cell color, font color, or conditional formatting rules, providing more flexibility in organizing your data.

- Undo and Revert: If you make a mistake or want to revert to the original order, you can use the "Undo" feature or sort the data range back to its original order.
- Sorting Connected Data: When sorting a range of data that includes connected cells, make sure to select the entire range to maintain data integrity. Otherwise, the sorting may break the connections between the cells.

FILTERING DATA WITH FILTERS AND FILTER VIEWS

Filtering data is a powerful technique that allows you to extract specific subsets of data based on certain criteria. Google Spreadsheets provides two primary methods for filtering data: filters and filter views. In this chapter, we will explore how to use these tools effectively to filter and analyze data in a Google Spreadsheet. By mastering the art of filtering data, you can easily uncover valuable insights, identify trends, and focus on the information that matters most.

Using Filters:

Filtersin Google Spreadsheet allow you to quickly and easily display only the data that meets specific criteria. Here's how to use filters effectively:

1. Enable Filters:
- Select the data range you want to filter.
- Go to Data > Create a filter.
2. Apply Filters:
- Once filters are enabled, you will see drop-down arrows next to the column headers.
- Click on the dropdown arrow for a specific column to see the filter options.
- Choose the desired filter criteria, such as text, number, date, or custom conditions.
3. Multiple Filters:

- You can apply filters to multiple columns simultaneously to create complex filter combinations.
- Use the filter options in each column to refine the data displayed.
4. Clear Filters:
- To remove filters and display the full dataset again, go to Data > Turnoff filters.

Filter Views:

Filter Views provide a more advanced and flexible way to filter and analyze data in a Google Spreadsheet. Here's how to use filter views effectively:

1. Create a filtered view:
- Select the data range you want to filter.
- Goto Data > Filter Views > Create a new filter view.
2. Customize Filters:
- In the Filter View toolbar, you can apply filters to different columns and specify the filter criteria.
- You can also add multiple filter conditions within a column to create more refined views.
3. Save and Manage Filter Views:
- Filter views can be saved for future use or shared with others.
- Use the "Save" button in the Filter View toolbar to save the current view.
- To manage filter views, go to Data > Filter Views > Manage filter views.
4. Switching between filter views:
- You can easily switch between different filter views to analyze the data from different perspectives.
- Go to Data > Filter Views and choose the desired filter view from the list.

Advanced Filtering Techniques

1. **Sorting with Filters:**
- Filters can be used in combination with sorting to further refine your data analysis.
- Apply filters to the desired columns, and then sort the filtered data based on specific criteria.
2. Conditional Formatting with Filters:
- Conditional formatting can be applied to filter data to highlight specific patterns or trends.
- Use formatting rules to dynamically change the cell formatting based on the applied filters.
3. Advanced Filter Conditions:
- Google Spreadsheet allows you to create custom filter conditions using formulas and logical operators.
- Use advanced filter conditions to filter databased on complex criteria and perform sophisticated data analysis.

USING DATA VALIDATION TO CONTROL INPUT

Users of Google Sheets have the ability to control the types of data that they can enter into a cell or range of cells in a sheet through the use of a tool called Data Validation. This function can be found in Google Sheets. An error message will be displayed by Google Sheets in the event that a user attempts to enter data that does not satisfy the validation criteria. This will prevent the user from entering the wrong data. This can be helpful in preventing errors and ensuring the accuracy of the data and formulae on your spreadsheet. For instance, if you use data validation, you can restrict the kinds of data that can be entered into a cell by setting rules, such as the following examples:

- A predetermined numerical range, such as restricting the allowed digits to be between 1 and 100 only
- A list of predefined values or text strings, for example, only allows the values "Yes" or "No" to be entered.
- A certain date range, such as restricting the accepted dates to those that fall within a defined time frame

You may make your analysis, a KPI dashboard, or a financial model more efficient and valid by utilizing the Data Validation tool. This allows you to avoid overlooking unusual data or modifying your model or formulas to conform to new input types. To be more explicit, for example, Data Valid at ion can be helpful in the following situations:

- You want to make sure that the data entry in a list is consistent from the very beginning to the very end.
- You would like to place restrictions on the data style or the data input (for example, a certain range of numbers: 1- 10).
- You will need to generate a drop-down menu that provides users with certain option

Enabling Data Validation

To start using data validation, follow these steps:

1. Select the cell(s):
- Click on the cell(s) where you want to apply data validation.
2. Open the Data Validation Dialog:
- Go to Dat a > Data Validation.
3. Define validation criteria:
- In the data validation dialog box, choose the criteria you want to apply to the selected cell(s).
- Options include whole numbers, decimals, dates, text length, custom formulas, and more.
4. Set Validation Rules:
- Specify the validation rules, such as between specific values, equal to a certain value, or based on a custom formula.

5. Input Message (Optional):
- You can provide an input message to guide users when entering data in the validated cell(s).
- The message appears as a small pop-up when the cell(s) are selected.
6. Error Message (Optional):
- Set an error message that displays when users enter invalid data in the validated cell(s).
- The error message helps users understand the validation criteria and correct their input.

Common Use Cases for Data Validation

Data validation can be applied in various scenarios to control input and improve data quality. Here are some common use cases:

1. Restricting Numeric Values:
- Set validation criteria to allow only whole numbers or specific ranges of decimal values.
- This is useful when you want to ensure users enter numeric data within a specified range.
2. Limiting Text Length:
- Define a maximum character limit for text input in a cell.
- This helps maintain consistency and prevents users from exceeding specified text lengths.
3. Selecting from a List
- Create a drop-down list of pre-defined options using data validation.
- Users can choose from the provided list, ensuring data consistency and reducing input errors.
4. Validating Dates:
- Specify date formats and ranges to ensure users enter dates correctly.
- This prevents invalid date entries and maintains data integrity.
5. Custom Formulas:
- Utilize custom formulas to create advanced validation rules.
- This allows for more complex validations, such as verifying combinations of values or comparing data across cells.

Data Validation Tips and Best Practices

Consider the following tips and best practices when working with data validation:

1. Use input messages:
- Provide clear instructions or hints to guide users when entering data.
- Input messages help users understand the expected input format or specific requirements.
2. Error Messages:

- Create meaningful error messages to alert users when they enter invalid data.
- Clearly explain the validation criteria and suggest corrections.
3. Apply to Multiple Cells:
- You can apply data validation rules to multiple cells at once by selecting a range of cells.
- This saves time and ensures consistency across multiple cells.
4. Protecting Data Validation Settings:
- To maintain data integrity, protect data validation settings to prevent others from modifying or deleting the validation rules.
5. Conditional Data Validation:
- Use formulas in data validation criteria to create conditional rules.
- This allows validation to be based on other cell values or complex conditions.

ORGANIZING AND MANAGING SHEETS AND TABS

Google Spreadsheet offers a versatile environment for managing and organizing data, allowing you to work with multiple sheets and tabs within a single spreadsheet file. Proper organization and management of sheets and tabs can greatly enhance your productivity, improve data accessibility, and simplify collaboration. In this section, we will explore various techniques and best practices for organizing and managing sheets and tabs in Google Spreadsheets.

Creating and Renaming Sheets

1. Creating a New Sheet
- To create a new sheet, click on the "+" button at the bottom left corner of the Google Spreadsheet interface.
- Alternatively, right-click on an existing sheet tab and select "Insert sheet" from the context menu.
2. Renaming a Sheet
- Double-click on the sheet tab you wish to rename and enter a newname.
- Alternatively, right-click on the sheet tab and select "Rename" from the context menu.

Rearranging and Grouping Sheets

1. Rearranging Sheets:
- To change the order of sheets, click on a sheet tab and drag it to the desired position.
- The new position will be indicated by a vertical line.
2. Grouping Sheets:
- Grouping sheets allow you to organize related sheets together, making them easier to navigate and manage.
- To group sheets, select the sheets you want to group by holding down the Ctrl or Cmd key and clicking on the sheet tabs.

- Right-click on one of the selected sheet tabs and choose "Group" from the context menu.
- Grouped sheets can be collapsed or expanded by clicking on the small triangle icon next to the group name.

Changing Tab Colors

1. Changing tab color:
- To differentiate between sheets or highlight important sheets, you can change the tab color.
- Right-click on a sheet tab and select "Tab color" from the context menu.
- Choose a color from the color palette or select "Cust om color" for more options.

Hiding and Unhiding Sheets

1. Hiding Sheets:
- To hide a sheet, right-click on its tab and select "Hide sheet" from the context menu.
- Hidden sheets are not visible in the sheet tabs but can still be accessed and unhidden.
2. Unhiding Sheets:
- To unhide a hidden sheet, click on the arrow icon located to the right of the last visible sheet tab.
- A list of hidden sheets will be displayed, allowing you to select and unhide specific sheets.

Protecting Sheets and Tabs

1. Protecting Sheets:
- To protect a sheet from accidental changes, go to the "Data" menu and select "Protect sheets and ranges."
- Set the permissions for the protected sheet, such as allowing specific users to edit or view the sheet.
2. Hiding and Protecting Tabs:
- To hide and protect tabs, you can utilize Google Spreadsheet add-ons or scripts.
- These tools allow you to customize the visibility and access permissions for specific tabs within a spreadsheet.

Using Tab Summaries and Table of Contents

1. Tab Summaries:
- Create a summary sheet that provides an overview of the contents and structure of your spreadsheet.
- Use this sheet to list the names, descriptions, or other relevant information about each sheet or tab.
2. Table of Contents:

- Create a table of contents sheet that serves as a navigation tool within your spreadsheet.
- Link the table of contents to each sheet or tab, making it easier to navigate between different sections of your spreadsheet.

CHAPTER 7: COLLABORATION AND SHARING FEATURES

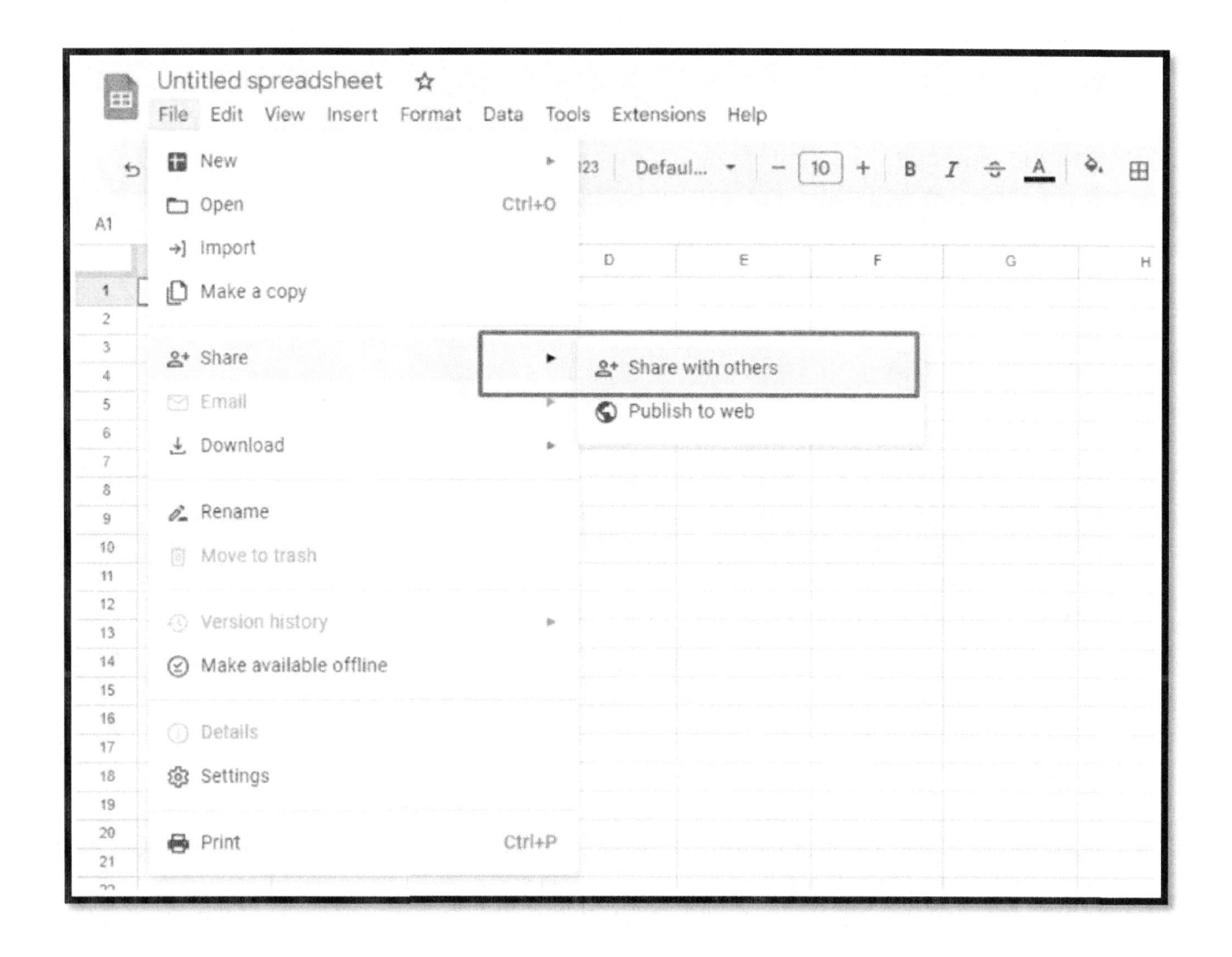

SHARING SPREADSHEETS AND COLLABORATING WITH OTHERS

Google Spreadsheets offers powerful collaboration features that enable multiple users to work on the same spreadsheet simul-taneously, share data securely, and facilitate seamless collaboration. In this chapter, we will explore various aspects of collabora-tion and data sharing in Google Spreadsheets, empowering you to collaborate effectively with others and enhance productivity.

Sharing Spreadsheets

1. Sharing Options:
- To share a spreadsheet with others, click on the "Share" button located in the top-right corner of the Google Spreadsheet interface.
- Specify the email addresses or Google accounts of the individuals you want to share the spreadsheet with.
- Choose the appropriate sharing permissions, such as view, comment, or edit access.

2. Sharing Links:
- Google Spreadsheets allows you to generate sharing links that can be shared with anyone, even without a Google account.
- You can control the level of access granted to users via the sharing link, such as view-only or edit access.
3. Sharing Settings:
- In the sharing settings, you can manage and modify the access permissions of individual users or groups.
- You can also revoke access, change ownership, and set expiration dates for shared links.

Collaborative Editing

1. Simultaneous Editing:
- Google Spreadsheets allows multiple users to edit the same spreadsheet simultaneously.
- Each user's edits are highlighted in real-time, making it easy to track changes and collaborate effectively.
2. Collaborative Features:
- Collaborators can leave comments, suggest edits, and engage in discussions within the spreadsheet.
- Use the "Insert Comment" option to provide feedback or ask questions about specific cells or ranges.
3. Revision History:
- The revision history feature tracks all changes made to the spreadsheet, including who made the changes and when.
- You can access the revision history by going to File > Version History > See Version History.

Notifications and Alerts

1. Email Notifications:
- Google Spreadsheets can send email notifications to inform collaborators about changes, comments, or suggestions.
- Collaborators can choose their notification preferences to stay updated on the spreadsheet's activity.
2. Alerts and Notification Rules:
- Use the "Notifications Rules" opt ion to set up custom alerts based on specific conditions or changes in the spreadsheet.
- You can receive notifications when specific cells are modified or when certain criteria are met.

Importing and Exporting Data

1. Importing Data:

- Google Spreadsheets supports importing data from various sources, including CSV files, Excel spreadsheets, and databases.
- Use the "File" menu and select the appropriate import option to bring data into your spreadsheet.

2. Exporting Data:
- You can export your spreadsheet to different file formats, such as PDF, Excel, CSV, and more.
- Go to File > Download and choose the desired format to export the spreadsheet.

Collaboration Best Practices

1. Clear Communication:

Establish clear communication channels with your collaborators, ensuring everyone is aware of their roles and responsibilities.

2. Version Control:
- Encourage collaborators to utilize the revision history feature and provide clear documentation of changes made to the spreadsheet.
3. Data Security:
- Be mindful of sensitive data and ensure proper access controls are in place to protect confidential information.
4. Regular Backups:
- Regularly backup your spreadsheet to prevent data loss or accidental changes.

Sharing spreadsheets and collaborating with others can be done efficiently using various tools and platforms. Here are a few common methods for sharing and collaborating on spreadsheets:

1. Google Sheets:

Google Sheets is a cloud-based spreadsheet tool that allows real-time collaboration. To share a spreadsheet, you can invite others by enter-ing their email addresses and specifying the access permissions (view only, comment, or edit). Collaborators can work on the spreadsheet simultaneously, make changes, leave comments, and see each other's edits in real-time.

2. Microsoft Excel Online:

Microsoft Excel Online, part of Microsoft 365, provides similar functionality to Google Sheets. You can upload your Excel spreadsheet to OneDrive or SharePoint and then share it with others. Multiple users can work on the spreadsheet simultaneously and see changes in real time.

3. Office Suite Applications:

If you use desktop-based spreadsheet applications like Microsoft Excel or LibreOffice Cale, you can still collaborate by using shared file locations such as OneDrive, Dropbox, or a shared network drive. Ensure that the file is accessible to the collaborators and that everyone is working on the latest version.

4. Collaboration Add-ons:

Some spreadsheet tools offer collaboration add-ons or plugins that enhance collaboration capabilities. For example, in Google Sheets, you can use add-ons like" Collaborative Comments" or "Track Changes" to facilitate collaboration and document revision.

5. Version Control:

When collaborating on spreadsheets, it's important to keep track of changes and maintain version control. This ensures that you can revert to previous versions if needed. Some platforms, like Google Sheets, automatically maintain revision histories, allowing you to re- view changes made by collaborators and restore earlier versions.

6. Communication Tools:

To enhance collaboration, it's helpful to use communication tools alongside spreadsheet sharing. Tools like Slack, Microsoft Teams, or project management platforms enable real-time discussions, file sharing, and task coordination, making it easier to collaborate effectively.

MANAGING AND REVIEWING CHANGES

When it comes to finding an easy-to-use and cost-effective platform for team communication, Google Sheets is the option that everyone turns to first. This tool is especially helpful for undertaking tasks that require gathering, storing, and analyzing data in a manner that is both straightforward and time-effective.

Nevertheless, when working together on the same file, one of the most typical problems that can a rise is the loss of essential data or the inability to revert to an earlier version of the file. In contrast to Google Docs and other desktop productivity tools, Google Sheets does not include a dedicated function that may monitor changes made to a document.

You will learn how to track changes in Google Sheets using a variety of approaches, such as notification rules, version history, conditional formatting, and tracking changes in a specific cell, throughout the course of this tutorial.

How can I keep track of changes using the notification rules in Google Sheets?

You are able to define notification rules in Google Sheets according to the type of change and the frequency of notification if you want to ensure that you are kept up to date on any modifications that are made to your sheets. You can monitor changes in Google Sheets by using notifications in the manner outlined here.

1. Launch Google Sheets and navigate to the Tools menu, then select Notification rules.
2. Selecting "Any changes are made" under "Set notification rules" will allow you to take advantage of the same capabilities that are made available by the "Track Changes" feature in other products. You may adjust the frequency of alerts by going to the "Notify me with..."section. Within this window, I have chosen the "Email - right away" option. When you are finished, click the "Save" button.
3. Setting your notification rules to "Emai l - daily digest" is something that were commend doing in the event that you wish to pre- vent receiving an excessive amount of emails.
4. As soon as you save the rule, Google Sheets will ask you whether you want to "Edit " or "Delete " the rules that you have already set up. You are able to include more rules in this section. When you are done, click the "Done" button.

How Can I Keep Track of Changes Using the Version History in Google Sheet s?

Another option for keeping track of changes in Google Sheets is to use the "Version history" feature. You will now be able to access all of the information regarding the change, including details such as when it was made and who made it.

1. Select "See version history" from the "File" menu, then" Version history."
2. You will be able to view all prior versions on the "Version history" panel, which is located to the far right of the screen. This panel also displays the date, the time, and the user who was responsible for the changes.
3. To see all of the versions in their entirety, click on the arrow to the left of the information that says" drop down," which will enlarge the data for the version history.
4. You can save a specific version of the file and then rename it to have full control over the version. By default, Google Sheets gives each version a name that is based on the date and time it was created. You may easily rename it by double-clicking on the name of the version in the menu.
5. Take into account that Google Sheets will only let you save up to 15 different versions of your work in total.
6. If you select an older version of your file, Google will give you the option to restore it, as well as rename it or make a copy of it. You can also choose to make a copy of it. Todo this, click on the icon that looks like a plus sign ("+"), which is located to the right of the version date and time.

Now that you know how to utilize the "Version history" tool, let's have a look at how to use the feature that Google just recently added to track changes in a particular cell.

How Can I Monitor the Changes Made to A Particular Cell in Google Sheets?

There is a function integrated into Google Sheets that will allow you to monitor changes made to a particular cell. You can get to it quite quickly by doing it this way.

1. Right-click on the cell you want to track changes for, and then pick "Show edit history" from the drop-down menu that appears after you make the selection.
2. To view the changes that have been made to the cell, simply click on the arrows to navigate back and forth through the history of those changes.
3. You can gain access to the pertinent information associated with a certain alteration in a matter of simple actions.

This function is especially helpful for cells that contain specific formulae or more sensitive information because it hides the formulae and information from view.

USING COMMENTS AND NOTES FOR COMMUNICATION

Comments and notes in Google Sheets are valuable tools for communication and collaboration within a spreadsheet. Here's how you can use comm ents and notes effectively:

1. **Adding Comments:**
- Select the cell or range where you want to add a comment.
- Right-click on the selected area and choose "Insert comment. "Alternatively, you can use the keyboard shortcuts Ctrl+ Alt +M(Windows) or Command +Option+ M(Mac).
- A comment box will appear on the side of the cell. Enter your comment in the text box.
- You can also mention collaborators in the comment by using the "@" symbol followed by their email address. They will receive an email notification about the comment.

2. **Resolving and Editing Comments:**
- To resolve a comment, click on the comment box and then click the "Resolve " button (represented by a checkmark).
- Resolved comments are still visible in the spreadsheet but appear minimized. You can expand them to view the resolved comment thread if needed.
- To edit a comment, click on the comment box, make the necessary changes, and click outside the box to save the edits.

3. **Replying to Comments:**
- Comments can spark discussions and conversations among collaborators. To reply to a comment, click on the comment box and enter your response.
- Collaborators can reply to comments, creating a threaded discussion within the comment box.
- Replies are nested beneath the original comment, making it easy to follow the conversation.

4. **Notifying Collaborators:**

- When you add a comment and mention a collaborator using the "@" symbol, they will receive an email notification with your comment.
- Collaborators can respond to the comment directly via email or by accessing the spreadsheet.

5. **Viewing and Navigating Comments:**
- To view comments within a spreadsheet, you can click on the cell containing the comment, and the comment box will appear.
- Alternatively, you can access all comments in the spreadsheet by clicking on the "Comments" button in the toolbar at the top-right corner. This opens a sidebar displaying all the comments in the spreadsheet, organized by sheet.

6. **Adding Notes:**
- Notes are another way to add information or explanations to cells in a more concise manner than comments.
- To add a note, right-click on the cell, select" Insert note," and enter your note.
- Notes appear as small yellow rectangles in the corner of the cell. Hovering over the cell will display the note.

PUBLISHING AND EMBEDDING SHEETS IN DIFFERENT FORMATS

We will explore the various options available for publishing and embedding Google Sheets in different formats.

1. **Publish to the Web:**

Publishing a Google Sheet to the web allows you to share it as a web page or embed it on other platforms. Here's how to do it:

- Open the Google Sheet you want to publish and navigate to the "File" menu.
- Choose "Publish to the Web," and a dialog box will appear.
- Select the sheet(s) you want to publish and choose the desired publishing options.
- Click the "Publish " button, and you'll be provided with a link to the published web page or an embed code for use in websites or blogs.

2. **Embedding Sheets in Websites or Blogs:**

Google Sheets can be embedded directly into websites or blogs, allowing visitors to view and interact with the spreadsheet without leaving the webpage. Follow these steps to embed a Google Sheet:

- Publish the Google Sheet to the web using the steps mentioned above.
- Copy the embed code provided after publishing.
- Open the HTML source code of your website or blog where you want to embed the sheet.
- Paste the embed code into the appropriate location within the HTML code.
- Save and update the webpage, and the embedded sheet will be displayed to visitors.

3. Exporting as PDF or Excel:

Google Sheets allows you to export your spreadsheet in different formats, including PDF and Excel. Here's how to export a Google Sheet:

- Open the Google Sheet you want to export and navigate to the "File" menu.
- Choose the "Download" option and select the desired format, such as PDF or Excel.
- The file will be downloaded to your device, and you can save it or share it as needed.

4. Publishing as CSV or TSV:

If you need to share your data in a simple, comma-separated (CSV) or t ab -separated (TSV) form at, Google Sheets makes it easy. Follo w these steps:

- Open the Google Sheet s and navigate to the "File" menu.
- Choose the "Down load" option and select either "Comma-separated values" or "Tab separated values."
- The file will be downloaded in the chosen format, which can then be shared or imported into other applications.

5. Link Sharing and Access Permissions:

Apart from the publishing options, Google Sheets also provides link sharing and access permissions for collaborative work. These features allow you to control who can view, comment on, or edit the spreadsheet. To set access permissions:

- Open the Google Sheet and click the "Share" button in the top-right comer.
- Enter the email addresses of the collaborators and choose their access permissions (view, comment, or edit).
- Collaborators can access the shared sheet through the provided link or by logging into their Google accounts.

CHAPTER 8: ADVANCED DATA ANALYSIS

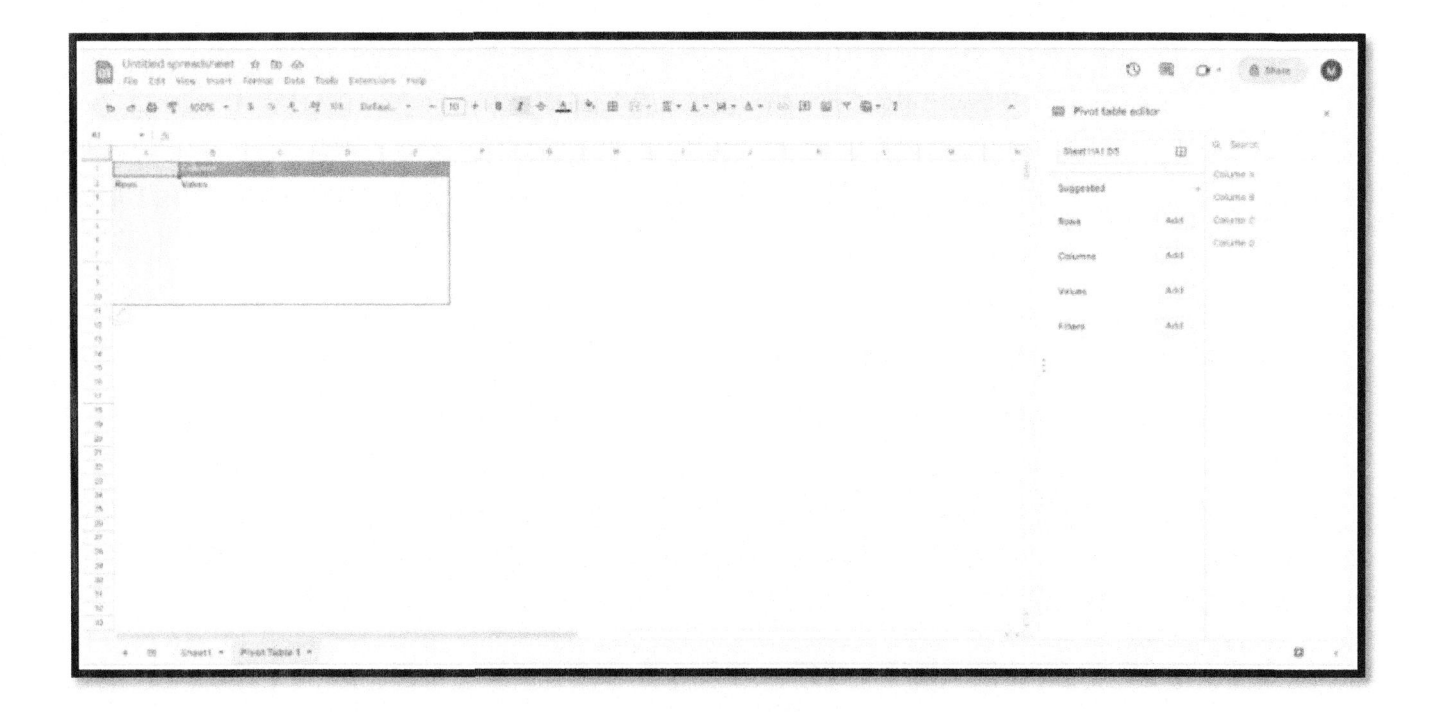

PIVOT TABLES: ANALYZING DATA FROM DIFFERENT PERSPECTIVES

Advanced data analysis techniques in Google Sheets offer several benefits that can significantly enhance your data analysis capa-bilities. Here are some key advantages:

1. Efficient Data Summarization and Visualization:

Advanced techniques like pivot tables allow you to summarize and aggregate large datasets quickly. Instead of manually sorting and calculating data, you can create pivot tables to obtain meaningful insights and visualize the data in a concise and understandable format. This saves time and effort, especially when dealing with complex datasets.

2. Enhanced Data Accuracy and Integrity:

Utilizing data validation features in Google Sheets helps ensure data accuracy and integrity. By setting validation rules and constraints, you can prevent incorrect or inconsistent data entries. This leads to cleaner datasets and reduces the risk of errors or inaccuracies in your analysis.

3. Quick Identification of Patterns and Trends:

Conditional formatting in Google Sheets enables you to visually highlight patterns, trends, and outliers within your data. By applying formatting rules based on specific conditions, you can easily identify important datapoints or areas of interest. This visual representation helps in detecting patterns or deviations that might not be immediately evident in raw data.

4. Statistical Insights and Analysis:

Google Sheets provides a comprehensive range of built-in statistical functions that enable you to perform advanced calculations and analysis. These functions help you derive statistical insights from your data, such as calculating averages, sums, standard deviations, cor-relations, and more. With these statistical in sights, you can make informed decisions, identify relationships between variables, and quan-tify the impact of different factors.

5. Predictive Analytics and Forecasting:

The regression analysis tools available in Google Sheets, such as the "trend" and "forecast" functions, allow you to perform predictive analytics and forecasting. By fitting a line to your data, you can estimate future values and make predictions based on the relationship be- tween variables. This capability is valuable for trend analysis, demand forecasting, and planning future actions or strategies.

6. Optimization and Decision-Making Support:

The Solver add-on in Google Sheets offers optimization capabilities, allowing you to find the best solution given specific constraints. This tool is valuable for scenarios where you need to maximize or minimize a target value by adjusting variables while adhering to specific lim-itations. Solver can help optimize resource allocation, production planning, scheduling, and other decision-making processes.

7. Flexible Data Manipulation and Extraction:

The Query Language in Google Sheets enables you to manipulate and extract data using SQL-like queries directly within your spreadsheet. This offers flexibility in data transformation, filtering, and joining multiple datasets for analysis. By leveraging the power of the query lan-guage, you can efficiently extract specific data subsets, apply conditions, aggregate data, and perform advanced data manipulations.

Pivot Tables

Pivot tables are a powerful tool in data analysis that allows you to summarize and analyze large sets of data from different perspectives. With pivot tables, you can quickly transform complex datasets into meaningful insights by rearranging, summarizing, and filtering data to focus on specific aspects of interest. In this step-by-step guide, we will walk you through the process of creating and using pivot tables effectively.

Step 1:

Prepare Your Data Before creating a pivot table; it's important to ensure your data is well organized and contains all the necessary informa-tion. Here are a few tips for preparing your data:

1. Arrange your data in a tabular format, with each column representing a specific attribute and each row representing a unique data entry.
2. Ensure that your data has column headers, as pivot tables rely on these headers to identify the attributes you want to analyze.
3. Remove any blank rows or columns from your dataset to avoid including unnecessary data in your pivot table.

Step 2:

Select your data range. Once your data is ready, select the entire range of data that you want to include in your pivot table. This range should cover all the relevant rows and columns.

Step 3:

Insert a Pivot Table In Microsoft Excel, navigate to the "Insert" tab and click on the "PivotTable" button. This will open the Create PivotTable dialog box. In other spreadsheet software or tools, the process might vary slightly, but the concept remains the same.

Step 4:

Choose Your Data Source In the Create PivotTable dialog box, verify that the "Select a table or range" option is selected. Make sure that the correct data range is automatically detected. If not, manually enter the correct data range or use the "Select Table" button to choose the range.

Step 5:

Decide the Pivot Table Location Next, choose where you want to place your pivot table. You can either create a new worksheet or select an existing one. Select the desired option and click "OK."

Step 6:

Design Your Pivot Table Now that you have inserted a pivot table, you need to design it according to your analytical requirements. Here's what you can do:

1. **Drag and drop fields:**

In the PivotTable Field List, you will find the column headers from your data source. Drag and drop these headers into different sections of the field list, such as rows, columns, values, or filters.

2. **Row and column labels:**

Dragging a field to the Rows section will create row labels while dragging a field to the Columns section will create column labels. This allows you to analyze your data across different dimensions.

3. Value calculation:

Dragging a numerical field to the Values section enables you to perform calculations like sum, average, count, etc., on that field.

4. Filtering:

Dragging a field to the Filters section allows you to apply filters to your data, narrowing down the scope of analysis.

Step 7:

Customize and Refine Your Pivot Table After designing your pivot table; you can customize and refine it further to enhance your analysis. Here are some additional options you can explore:

1. Formatting:

Apply formatting options to make your pivot table visually appealing and easy to interpret. Modify font styles, cell colors, borders, etc., as needed.

2. Sorting:

Sort the data within your pivot table to display it in a specific order, such as ascending or descending order, based on values, labels, or other criteria.

3. Calculated Fields:

Create new fields within the pivot table by using formulas or performing calculations based on existing fields.

4. Grouping:

Group data by specific attributes, such as dates or ranges of values, to summarize information at a higher level.

Step 8:

Refresh Your Pivot Table If your data changes or you add new data, you need to refresh your pivot table to update the analysis. In most spreadsheet software, you can simply right-click within the pivot table and select the "Refresh" or "Update" option.

USING ADVANCED FUNCTIONS FOR DATA ANALYSIS

Advanced functions for data analysis can help you gain deeper insights and perform complex calculations on your datasets. Here are some commonly used advanced functions and how to use them:

VLOOKUP (Vertical Lookup)

VLOOKUP is used to search for a value in the leftmost column of a table and retrieve a corresponding value from a specific column in that table. The syntax is as follows:

VLOOKUP (lookup_value, table_range, column_number,[range_lookup])

- lookup_value:

The value you want to search for.

- table_range:

The range of cells that contains the table you want to search in.

- column_number:

The column number(starting from 1)from which you want to retrieve the result.

- range_lookup:

[Optional]A logical value that specifies whether you want an exact match (false) or an approximate match (true or omitted).

HLOOKUP (Horizontal Lookup)

HLOOKUP works similarly to VLOOKUP, but it searches for a value in the top row of a table and retrieves a corresponding value from a specific row. The syntax is as follows:

HLOOKUP (lookup_value, table_range, row_number, [range _lookup])

- lookup_value:The value you want to search for.
- table_range: The range of cells that contains the table you want to search in.
- row_number: The row number (starting from 1) from which you want to retrieve the result.
- range_lookup:[Optional] Alogical value that specifies whether you want an exact match (false)or an approximate match (true or omitted).

SUMIF (Sum withCondition)

SUMIF allows you to add up values in a range that meets specific criteria. The syntax is as follows: SUMIF (range, criteria, [sum_range])

- range: The range of cells that you want to evaluate against the criteria
- criteria: The condition or criteria that the cells must meet to be included in the sum
- sum_range: [Optional] The range of cells that you want to sum. If omitted, the range argument is used as the sum_range.

COUNTIF (Count with Condition)

COUNTIF is used to count the number of cells in a range that meet specific criteria. The syntax is as follows: COUNTIF (rang e, criteria)

- range: The range of cells that you want to evaluate against the criteria
- criteria: the condition or criteria that the cells must meet to be counted.

AVERAGEIF (Average with Condition)

AVERAGEIF calculates the average of values in a range that meets specific criteria. The syntax is as follows: AVERAGEIF (range, criteria, [average_range])

- range: The range of cells that you want to evaluate against the criteria
- criteria: The condition or criteria that the cells must meet to be included in the average
- average_range: [Optional] The range of cells that you want to average. If omitted, the range argument is used as the average_range.

CREATING AND CUSTOMIZING CHARTS FOR DATA VISUALIZATION

Creating and customizing charts is a crucial part of data visualization. Charts help you present data in a visually appealing and easily un-derstandable format. Here are step-by-step instructions on creating and customizing charts:

Step 1:

Select your data. Before creating a chart, ensure that you have the data you want to visualize. Select the range of cells in your spreadsheet that contain the data you want to include in the chart. Include column headers if applicable.

Step2:

Insert a Chart: In most spreadsheet software, you can find the charting options in the "Insert" or "Charts" tab. Click on the chart type you want to create (e.g., column chart, line chart, pie chart) from the available options. This will insert a blank chart into your worksheet.

Step 3:

Choose a Chart Type: Select the specific chart type that best represents your data. Common chart types include column charts, bar charts, line charts, pie charts, scatter plots, and more. Consider the nature of your data and the insights you want to convey when choosing the ap- propriate chart type.

Step 4:

Customize the Chart: Once the chart is inserted, you can customize it to suit your preferences and make it more visually appealing. Here are some customization options to consider:

- **Chart Title:**

Add a descriptive title that summarizes the purpose or main message of the chart. This can be done by selecting the chart and entering the title in the provided textbox or through the chart options menu.

- **Axis Labels:**

Ensure that the x-axis (horizontal axis) and y-axis (vertical axis) have clear labels that explain the data being displayed. Customize the axis labels by double-clicking on them or accessing the options menu.

- **Data Labels:**

Add data labels to display specific values or percentages directly on the chart. This can be useful for highlighting key datapoints. You can enable data labels through the chart options or by right-clicking on the data series and selecting the appropriate option.

- **Legends:**

If you have multiple data series in your chart, adda legend to help viewers understand the different elements. Customize the legend posi-tion and appearance through the chart options or by right-clicking on the legend and accessing the settings.

- **Colors and Styles:**

Experiment with different color schemes, patterns, and styles to enhance the visual impact of your chart. Select the chart elements you want to modify and use the formatting options available in your software to change colors, line thickness, background, etc.

Step 5:

Data Series and Data Range You may want to adjust the data series or data range included in your chart. To do this, select the chart, and you will find options to modify the data source, add or remove series, or update the range. Ensure that your chart accurately represents the data you want to visualize.

Step 6:

Chart Layout and Formatting Continue customizing your chart by exploring additional layout and formatting options. This includes adjusting gridlines, adding trendlines, choosing different chart layouts, and exploring various formatting settings specific to your chart type. These options may vary depending on the software you are using.

Step 7:

Chart Interactivity and Animation (Optional) Some charting tools allow for interactivity and animation, which can enhance the user experience. Explore options to add interactive elements like tooltips, drill-down capabilities, or animation effects to make your chart more engaging and interactive.

Step 8:

Save and Share Your Chart Once you are satisfied with your chart, save your worksheet or export the chart as an image or PDF file. Consider the appropriate format for sharing the chart, such as embedding it in a presentation, including it in a report, or sharing it online.

PERFORMING STATISTICAL ANALYSIS IN GOOGLE SHEETS

The act of gathering and evaluating huge amounts of data is known as statistical analysis. The goal of statistical analysis is to discover patterns and gain insightful new perspectives.

Statistical analysts are employed in the business world to take raw data and discover correlations between variables in order to disclose patterns and trends to relevant stakeholders. Statistical analysts are responsible for making new scientific discoveries, improving the health of our communities, and influencing the decisions that are made in the commercial world. They work in a wide range of diverse sectors.

Data Entry and Organization:

Before delving into statistical analysis, it is essential to make certain that your data have been accurately recorded and structured within Google Sheets. It is important that each column be used to represent a distinct variable or trait and that each row be used to represent a single observation. Spend some time organizing and cleaning up your data in a suitable manner, getting rid of any duplicates, outliers, or inconsistent readings.

Statistics:

Descriptive statistics are statistics that describe your data by describing its most important qualities. Calculating numerous measure-ments, including the mean, median, mode, standard deviation, and variance, is made possible by a variety of in-built functions available in Google Sheets. When applied to the relevant data range, these functions, such as AVERAGE, MEDIAN, MODE, ST DEV, and VAR, provide immediate insights into the central tendency, variability, and distribution of the data.

Data visualization:

It allows us to gain a better understanding of the underlying patterns and relationships in the data by presenting it in graphical form. Bar charts, line graphs, scatter plots, and histograms are some of the several types of charts that can be created with Google

Sheets. You will be able to build attractive visual representations of your data by selecting the data range and selecting an appropriate chart type. This will make it possible for you to more easily evaluate and analyze the data.

Testing the Hypothesis:

Testing the hypothesis enables us to draw conclusions about a population based on a sample taken from that population. Google Sheets provides users with a number of different functions, such as TTEST, CHITEST, and ZTEST, that can be utilized to conduct a variety of hy-pothesis tests. Using these tests, you'll be able to determine if the differences or associations that you've found in your data are statistically significant or simply the result of random chance.

Analysis of Regression:

The analysis of regression enables us to comprehend the connection between the variables and to forecast the results. Under the "Data Analysis" add-on in Google Sheets, a powerful tool known as "Regression " is available to use. You will be able to execute linear regression with the assistance of this tool, which will enable you to calculate coefficients and intercepts as well as provide insight into the strength and direction of correlations between variables.

Pivot Tables:

Pivot tables are a useful tool for quickly summarizing and analyzing huge datasets. You can create pivot tables with ease using Google Sheets, which can assist you in analyzing data from a variety of perspectives. You may easily construct aggregated statistics such as counts, sums, averages, and percentages by dragging and dropping variables into rows, columns, and values. These statistics provide use-ful insights into your data. You can do this by dragging and dropping variables.

Add-Ons and User-Created Functions:

Google Sheets provides support for a wide variety of add-ons and user-generated functions that have been developed by the user commu-nity. The capabilities of Google Sheets can be expanded with the help of these add-ons, which provide extra statistical tools and function-alities. Add-ons can be found, for instance, for more advanced regression analysis, ANOVA, time series analysis, and even more types of analysis. Investigating the various add-ons that are accessible can improve the workflow of your statistical study.

CHAPTER 9: AUTOMATING WITH MACROS AND SCRIPTS

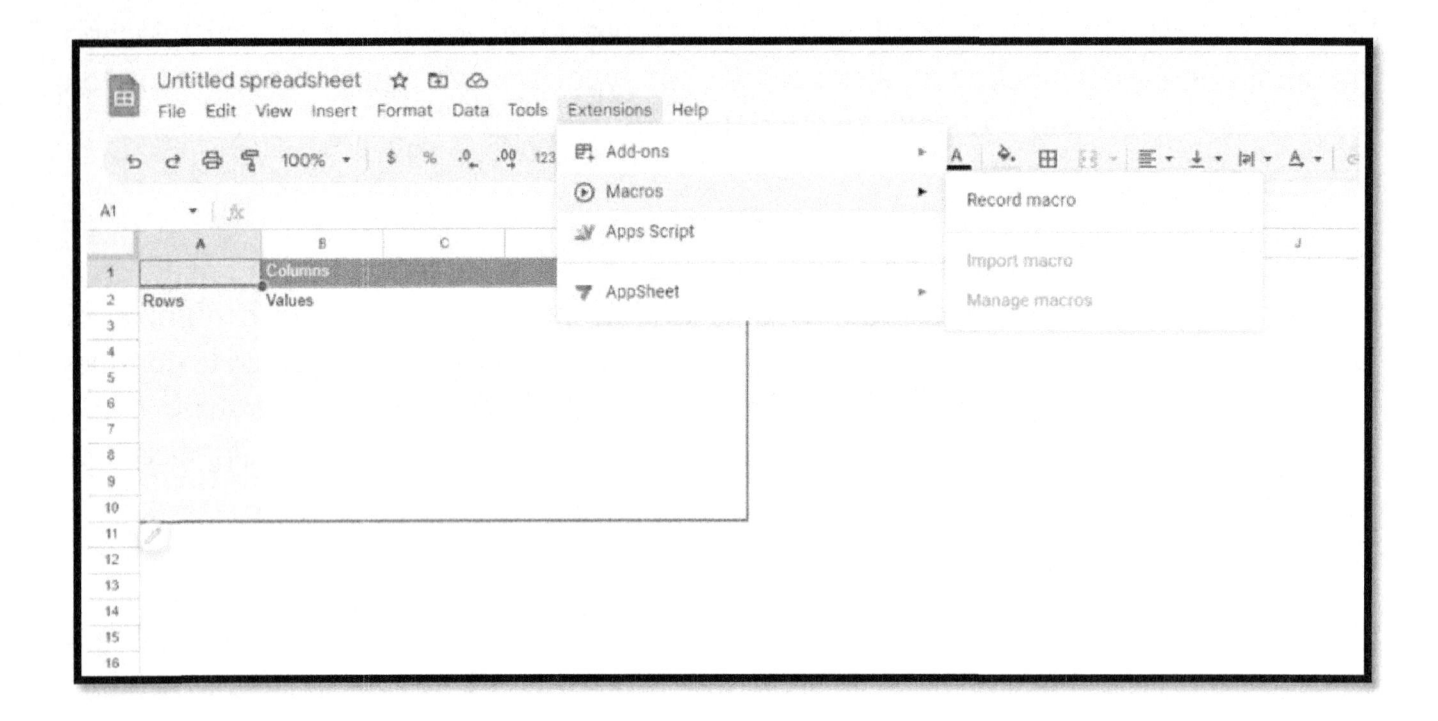

INTRODUCTION TO MACROS AND SCRIPTING IN GOOGLE SHEETS

In today's fast-paced world, time is of the essence. Th e ability to automate repetitive tasks can be a game-changer, allowing you to focus on more important aspects of your work. In this chapter, we will delve into the powerful world of macros and scripts in Google Sheets, unlocking their potential to save you time and effort. By mastering these automation techniques, you will become more efficient and productive in your spreadsheet endeavors.

UNDERSTANDING MACROS

Macros are a series of recorded actions that can be replayed to automate tasks in Google Sheets. They allow you to perform complex opera-tions with a single click or shortcut. Before diving into creating macros, it is important to understand the basics.

Recording Macros

To record a macro, navigate to the "Tools" menu in Google Sheets and select "Macros." Click on "Record Macro" to begin the recording process. You can then perform a series of actions, such as formatting cells, entering data, or applying formulas. Once you're done, click on the "Stop" button, and your macro is ready for use.

Managing Macros

Google Sheets provides options to manage your macros efficiently. You can rename, edit, or delete macros as needed. Additionally, you can assign shortcuts to your macros, making it even more convenient to execute them.

MACRO EDITING AND CUSTOMIZATION

While recording macros can be a quick way to automate tasks, sometimes you may need to tweak or customize the recorded actions to achieve the desired results. This section explores the editing and customization options available in Google Sheets.

Modifying Macro Code

After recording a macro, Google Sheets generates the corresponding Apps Script code. By accessing the code editor, you can make changes to the code, adding additional actions, conditional statements, or loops. This level of customization empowers you to create more sophisti-cated and tailored automation solutions.

Parameterizing Macros

To enhance the flexibility of your macros, you can add parameters. Parameters allow you to pass dynamic values to your macro, making it adaptable to different situations. For example, you can create a macro that prompts the user for input each time it is executed, enabling them to specify the range of cells to perform actions on.

GOOGLE APPS SCRIPT

Beyond the realm of macros, Google Apps Script takes automation in Google Sheets to the next level. Apps Script allows you to write cus-tom scripts using JavaScript, providing even greater control and functionality.

Introduction to Google Apps Script

Apps Script is a cloud-based scripting platform that integrates with various Google services, including Google Sheets. It allows you to automate tasks, create custom functions, and interact with external APIs. By harnessing the power of JavaScript, you can build robust and scalable automation solutions.

Creating Custom Functions

One of the standout features of Apps Script is the ability to create custom functions. Thesefunctions can be used in formulas within your spreadsheets, extending the built-in formula repertoire. With custom functions, you can perform advanced calculations, fetch data from external sources, or implement complex algorithms.

Interacting with External APIs

Apps Script provides seamless integration with external APIs, enabling you to fetch and manipulate data from various web services. You can retrieve real-time stock prices, access weather information, or interact with social media platforms. The possibilities are endless, limited only by the APis available and your creativity.

Advanced Automation Techniques

This final section covers advanced automation techniques that can take your mastery of Google Sheets to new heights.

Triggering Scripts

Google Sheets offers various triggers that can execute your scripts automatically. You can set up time-based triggers to run scripts at specific intervals or event-based triggers that respond to changes in the spreadsheet. By utilizing triggers effectively, you can create a fully automated workflow tailored to your needs.

Building Custom User Interfaces

With Apps Script, you can build custom user interfaces (UI) to enhance the user experience and simplify complex workflows. By creating custom menus, sidebars, or dialog boxes, you can provide intuitive interfaces for executing your automation solutions. These UI compo-nents can be integrated seamlessly into Google Sheets, making your automation efforts more user-friendly.

INTRODUCTION TO MACROS AND SCRIPTING IN GOOGLE SHEETS

In the world of spreadsheet software, Google Sheets stands out as a powerful and versatile tool for data manipulation and analysis. While the built-in features of Sheets provide a solid foundation, there are times when you need to go beyond the standard functionalities and automate tasks to save time and improve efficiency. This is where macros and scripting come into play. In this chapter, we will explore the fundamentals of macros and scripting in Google Sheets, empowering you to unlock the full potential of automation.

Understanding Macros

What are macros? Macros are a way to automate repetitive tasks in Google Sheets. They allow you to record a sequence of actions and replay them with a single click or a keyboard shortcut. Think of macros as a digital assistant that can perform a series of steps on your be- half, freeing up your time and energy for more important tasks.

The Benefits of Macros, The primary benefit of macros is their time-saving aspect. Instead of performing the same actions repeatedly, you can automate them with macros and execute them instantly. This not only saves time but also reduces the chances of errors that can occur during manual operations. Macros also promote consistency and accuracy in your spreadsheet work, ensuring that tasks are performed in the same way every time.

Creating and Managing Macros:

Recording Macros Creating macros in Google Sheets is a straightforward process. Start by navigating to the "Tools" menu and selecting "Macros." Choose "Record Macro" and proceed to perform the actions you want to automate. This can include formatting cells, applying formulas, or any other task you find yourself doing repeatedly. Once you're done, click on the "Stop" button, and your macro is ready to be used.

Assigning Macros to Shortcuts To make your macros even more accessible, you can assign keyboard shortcuts to them. This allows you to execute macros with a simple key combination, eliminating the need to navigate through menus. By customizing your shortcuts, you can create a streamlined workflow that matches your working style.

Managing Macros As your collection of macros grows, it becomes important to manage them effectively. Google Sheets provides options to rename, edit, or delete macros as needed. You can organize your macros into categories or folders, making it easier to find and use them when required. Proper management ensures that your macros remain a valuable asset in your spreadsheet arsenal.

Introduction to Scripting

What is scripting in Google Sheets? While macros offer a level of automation, scripting takes it to a whole new level. Scripting in Google Sheets involves writing code using the Google Apps Script language, which is based on JavaScript. This opens up a world of possibilities, enabling you to create custom functions, interact with external APis, and perform complex data manipulations.

Advantages of Scripting Scripting offers un paralleled flexibility and control over your spreadsheet automation. By writing custom scripts, you can create dynamic and sophisticated solutions tailored to your specific needs. Scripting allows you to automate co1n plex calculations, fetch data from external sources, and interact with other Google ser vices seamlessly. With scripting, the sky's the limit in terms of what you can achieve.

Getting Started with the Google Apps Script

Accessing Google Apps Script To start scripting in Google Sheets, navigate to the "Tools" menu and select "Script Editor." This opens up the integrated development environment (IDE), where you can write, test, and manage your scripts.

Basics of the Google Apps Script Google Apps Script uses JavaScript as its underlying language, making it accessible to a wide range of developers. If you're new to JavaScript, don't worry! The basics are easy to grasp, and Google provides ample documentation and resources to help you get started. You'll quickly find yourself harnessing the power of scripting in Google Sheets.

Writing Custom Functions One of the most powerful features of Google Apps Script is the ability to create custom functions. These functions can be used within your spreadsheet formulas, extending the built-in functionality of Sheets. With custom functions, you can perform advanced calculations, manipulate data, and create complex logic tailored to your specific requirements.

Creating Macros

Creating Macros and Enabling Macros To begin creating macros, ensure that the Google Sheets macro recorder is enabled. Go to the "Exten-sions" menu, select "Apps Script," and click on "Start Macro Recorder." This will activate the recorder, allowing you to capture your actions and convert them into a macro. Recording Macros Once the macro recorder is enabled, you can start recording your actions. Perform the series of steps that you want to automate, such as formatting cells, inserting formulas, or applying filters. The macro recorder will capture each action and generate the corresponding code.

Modifying Macro Code After recording the macro, you can fine-tune and customize the generated code to suit your specific requirements. Apps Script provides a comprehensive set of functions and methods to manipulate data, perform calculations, and interact with other Google services.

Running Macros

Running Macros Manually To execute a macro manually, navigate to the "Extensions" menu, select" Apps Script," and choose the desired macro from the list. The macro will then run and perform the defined actions on the active sheet or selected range.

Assigning Macros to Buttons For frequent and easy access, you can assign macros to buttons within your Google Sheets interface. This allows you to execute the macro with a single click, saving time and effort. To assign a macro to a button, go to the "Insert" menu, choose "Drawing," and create a button shape. Then, right-click on the button, select "Assign Script," and choose the desired macro from the list.

Running Macros Automatically To streamline your workflow even further, you can set macros to run automatically based on specific triggers. Triggers can be time-based, such as running the macro every hour or at a specific date and time, or event-based, such as running the macro when a particular cell is edited or when a sheet is opened. You can set triggers using the Apps Script editor by navigating to the "Edit" menu and selecting "Current project's triggers."

Best Practices for Macros Test and Debug Macros Before deploying macros in production, it is crucial to thoroughly test and debug them. Use sample data and verify that the macro performs the desired actions accurately. Debugging tools in Apps Script, such as the logger and breakpoints, can help identify and fix any issues.

Document Macros To ensure that macros remain accessible and maintainable, it is essential to document them properly. Include informa-tion about the purpose, inputs, outputs, and any limitations or dependencies of each macro. This documentation will be invaluable in the long run, especially when sharing macros with colleagues or revisiting them after a period of time.

Secure Macros As macros have the potential to modify data and perform actions on behalf of the user. It is essential to consider security aspects. Grant appropriate permissions to macros based on the required level of access, and be cautious when sharing macros with others to prevent unauthorized usage or data manipulation.

CUSTOMIZING APPS SCRIPT WITH MACROS

In the world of data management and analysis, customization plays a crucial role in maximizing productivity and efficiency. Google Sheets, with its versatile capabilities, allows users to create and run macros to automate repetitive tasks. However, to truly master Google Sheets, it is essential to go beyond the basic macros and explore the advanced customization options offered by Apps Script.

Apps Script is a JavaScript-based scripting language provided by Google that enables extensive customization and automation within various Google services, including Google Sheets. By utilizing Apps Script, you can extend the functionality of Google Sheets beyond the built-in features and create powerful and personalized macros.

Benefits of App Script By leveraging Apps Script, you can access a vast range of advanced functionalities and APis, allowing you to custom-ize macros according to your specific needs. Some benefits of using Apps Script include the ability to interact with external data sources, integrate with other Google services, create custom user interfaces, and implement complex logic and calculations.

Exploring Advanced Macro Customization

Accessing Apps Script Editor To begin customizing macros with Apps Script, navigate to the "Extensions" menu in Google Sheets and se-lect "Apps Script." This will open the Apps Script Editor, where you can write, modify, and manage scripts.

Extending the Functionality of Macros With Apps Script, you can enhance macros by incorporating advanced functionalities. For exam-ple, you can prompt the user for input using custom dialog boxes, manipulate data from external sources such as APis or databases, per- form complex calculations, and generate dynamic reports with custom formatting.

Leveraging Google Services and APis Apps Script allows you to interact with various Google services and APis, enabling seamless integra-tion between different platforms. You can, for instance, fetch data from Google Calendar, send emails through Gmail, access Google Drive files, or utilize the Google Translate API to perform language translations within your macros.

Creating Custom User Interfaces

Building Custom Dialog Boxes To enhance user interaction and provide a more intuitive experience, you can create custom dialog boxes within your macros using the Apps Script. These dialog boxes can include input fields, checkboxes, dropdown menus, and buttons, allow-ing users to input data or make selections that influence the macro's behavior.

Designing Sidebars and Add-ons Another way to customize the user interface is by creating custom sidebars or add-ons. Sidebars are docked panels that can display additional information or provide interactive features within the Google Sheets interface. Add-ons, on the other hand, are standalone applications that extend the functionality of Google Sheets. With Apps Script, you can design and deploy these custom interfaces to streamline workflows and provide a tailored experience for users.

Implementing Advanced Logic and Error Handling:

Utilizing Control Structures Apps Script provides a wide range of control structures, such as loops and conditionals, to implement ad-vanced logic within your macros. These structures allow you to iterate through data, perform conditional actions, and handle complex scenarios effectively.

Error Handling and Validation To ensure the robustness of your macros, it is crucial to implement error handling and data validation mechanisms. Apps Script offers various error handling techniques, such as try-catch blocks, to gracefully handle exceptions and provide

informative error messages to users. Additionally, you can validate user input, check for data integrity, and enforce business rules to pre- vent errors and ensure accurate macro execution.

Sharing and Collaborating on Customized Macros:

Sharing Macros with Others Apps Script provides seamless sharing options, allowing you to share your customized macros with others. The script grants specific individuals or groups access to your macros, controlling their level of permissions and collaboration. This en-ables effective teamwork and allows others to benefit from the macros you've created.

Leveraging Macro Libraries and Templates To further enhance collaboration and efficiency, you can create macro libraries or templates using Apps Script. Macro libraries contain reusable code snippets or functions that can be shared across different projects, saving time and effort. Templates, on the other hand, are pre-built macro frameworks that provide a starting point for specific tasks, enabling users to quickly customize and deploy macros for their unique requirements.

Integrating Google Sheets with Other Google Apps

Google Sheets is a powerful too lfor organizing and analyzing data. However, to truly harness its potential, it is essential to leverage the integration capabilities with other Google Apps. In this chapter, we will explore the seamless integration between Google Sheets and other Google apps, such as Google Docs, Google Slides, and Google Forms. By mastering these integrations, you can enhance collaboration, streamline workflows, and unlock new possibilities for data manipulation and presentation.

Integrating with Google Docs Linking data between Google Sheets and Google Docs Google Sheets allows you to link data directly to a Google Docs document. By using the "import Range()" function in Google Docs, you can pull data from specific ranges in a Google Sheets spreadsheet and dynamically update it as the data changes. This integration is particularly useful for generating reports, creating dynamic documents, or embedding live data within a document.

Embedding Google Sheets into Google Docs

In addition to linking data, you can embed an entire Google Sheets spreadsheet into a Google Docs document. This integration enables real- time collaboration and provides a convenient way to display data-rich content within a document. Changes made in the embedded spread- sheet will be reflected instantly in the document, ensuring data accuracy and consistency.

Integrating with Google Slides:

Importing Data from Google Sheets to Google Slides Google Sheets integration with Google Slides allows you to import data directly into a slide presentation. By using the "=import Range()"function in Google Slides, you can fetch data from a specific range in a Google Sheets

spreadsheet and display it in a slide. This integration simplifies the process of creating data-driven presentations and ensures that the data remains up-to-date.

Creating Charts and Graphs in Google Sheets for Google Slides Google Sheets offers a comprehensive set of charting and graphing capa-bilities. By creating charts in Google Sheets and linking them to a Google Slides presentation, you can easily visualize and present data in a visually appealing and dynamic manner. Any changes made to the data in Google Sheets will be automatically reflected in the charts within the Google Slides presentation.

Integrating with Google Forms

Using Google Sheets as a Data Source for Google Forms Google Forms is a powerful tool for creating surveys, quizzes, and feedback forms. With the integration between Google Sheets and Google Forms, responses collected through a Google Form can be automatically stored in a Google Sheets spreadsheet. This integration facilitates data analysis, allows for further data manipulation, and provides a centralized lo- cation for all form responses.

Automating Actions Based on Form Responses By utilizing the Apps Script, you can automate actions based on the responses received in a Google Form. For example, you can set up a script that sends email notifications, generates personalized reports, or triggers specific actions based on the form responses stored in Google Sheets. This integration adds a layer of automation and enhances the functionality of both Google Sheets and Google Forms.

Collaboration and Sharing

Sharing Google Sheets with Other Google App Users One of the significant advantages of using Google Apps is the seamless collaboration and sharing capabilities. You can easily share Google Sheets with others, granting them various levels of access, such as view-only, edit, or comment permissions. This collaboration allows for real-time collaboration, feedback, and data analysis among team members, improv-ing productivity and efficiency.

Version History and Revision Control

Google Sheets offers version history and revision control features, allowing you to track changes made to a spreadsheet over time. This functionality is particularly useful when collaborating with others on a document. You can view previous versions, compare changes, and even revert to an earlier version if needed. These features ensure data integrity and provide a comprehensive audit trail of modifications made to the spreadsheet.

CHAPTER 10: PRODUCTIVITY TIPS AND EFFICIENCY HACKS

KEYBOARD SHORTCUTS FOR FASTER NAVIGATION AND EDITING

As a powerful tool for data management and analysis, Google Sheets offers a wide range of features and functionalities. To become a master of Google Sheets, it is crucial to leverage tips and tricks that can enhance your productivity and efficiency. In this chapter, we will explore a variety of techniques, shortcuts, and best practices that will help you work smarter and accom-plish more with Google Sheets.

Data Entry and Navigation

Auto Fill and Auto Complete Save time and reduce errors by utilizing the Auto Fill and Auto Complete features in Google Sheets. Auto Fill allows you to quickly populate a series of cells with a pattern or sequence, such as dates, numbers, or text. Auto Complete suggests and completes your entries based on existing data in the column, minimizing manual typing and ensuring consistency.

Custom Sorting and Filtering Efficiently organize and analyze data by utilizing the sorting and filtering capabilities in Google Sheets. Customize the sorting order based on specific criteria, such as numerical or alphabetical, and apply multiple levels of sorting to sort data in a hierarchical manner. Use filters to display only the relevant databased on specified conditions, making it easier to focus on specific sub- sets of data.

Navigating and Selecting Data Master the art of navigating and selecting data in Google Sheets to streamline your workflow. Utilize key- board short cuts like the Ctrl+ Arrow keys to move quickly through large datasets. Use Ctrl+ A to select entire columns or rows and Shift+ Ar - row keys to select ranges of cells. Double-clicking the edge of a cell allows you to auto-fit the width or height of the column or row.

Formatting and Conditional Formatting

Conditional Formatting Make your data visually impactful and easier to interpret by using conditional formatting. Apply custom for- matting rules based on specified conditions to highlight cells, such as color-coding based on values, applying data bars or color scales, or adding icon sets. Conditional formatting provides visual cues that facilitate data analysis and understanding.

Cell Formatting Shortcuts Save time and effort by utilizing cell formatting shortcuts in Google Sheets. Use Ctrl+ Shift +1 to apply the default number format, Ctrl+Shift+4 to apply the currency format, and Ctrl +Shift +5 to apply the percentage format. These shortcuts allow you to quickly format cells without navigating through the formatting menus.

Using Format Painter The Format Painter tool is a handy feature in Google Sheets that allows you to quickly copy formatting from one cell or range of cells and apply it to other cells. Simply select the cell with the desired formatting, click on the Format Painter button, and then click on the cells where you want to apply the formatting. This feature saves time and ensures consistency in formatting across your spreadsheet.

Formulas and Functions

Using Named Ranges Simplify your formulas and improve readability by using named ranges. Instead of referring to cell ranges using coordinates, assign meaningful names to ranges. This makes formulas more intuitive and easier to understand, especially in complex spreadsheets.

Utilizing Array Formulas, Array formulas allow you to perform calculations on multiple cells simultaneously, saving time and reducing the need for repetitive formulas. By enclosing your formula in curly brackets (), you can apply it to an entire range of cells at once. Array formulas are particularly useful for performing calculations across multiple rows or columns of data.

Using Functions for Data Manipulation Google Sheets offers a vast array of built-in functions for data manipulation and analysis. Famil-iarize yourself with commonly used functions such as SUM, AVERAGE, COUNT, IF, VLOOKUP, and QUERY. These functions enable you to perform calculations, extract specific data, and manipulate your data efficiently.

Collaboration and Efficiency

Real-ti me Collaboration Leverage the power of real-time collaboration in Google Sheets to work efficiently with team members. Share your spreadsheet with collaborators, assign different levels of access, and work on the same sheet simultaneously. Utilize the chat feature to communicate and discuss changes directly within the spreadsheet.

Revision Hist or y a n d Comments Track changes made to your spreadsheet using the revision history feature. View previous versions, see who made specific changes, and revert to earlier versions if needed. Additionally, use comments to provide feedback, ask questions, or leave notes for yourself or collaborators within the spreadsheet.

Customizing Keyboard Shortcuts Personalize your Google Sheets experience by customizing keyboard shortcuts. Access the "Keyboard Shortcuts" option in the "Help" menu and define your preferred shortcuts for frequently used functions. This customization saves time and enhances your workflow by allowing you to perform actions with a few keystrokes.

Keyboard Shortcuts for Faster Navigation and Editing

Navigating Sheets and Cells

Moving Between Cells Effortlessly navigate between cells using keyboard shortcuts. Use the arrow keys to move one cell at a time in the respective direction. To jump to the beginning or end of a row or column, press Ct r! +Left, Right, Up, or Down. Pressi ng Ctr! +Home will take you to the top-left cell of the sheet.

Jumping Between Sheets When working with multiple sheets within a Google Sheets file, quickly switch between them using Ctrl+ Page Up or Page Down. This shortcut allows you to navigate seamlessly and access different sheets without having to manually click on the sheet tabs.

Selecting Cells and Ranges Selecting cells or ranges efficiently is key to working with data effectively. Use the Shift+ Arrow keys to select a range of cells in a specific direction. To select an entire row or column, press Ctrl +Spacebar or Shift +Spacebar, respectively. Shift +Ctrl+ Ar-row keys allow you to quickly select cells in a contiguous range.

Editing and Formatting

Entering Dat a Speed up data entry with key board short cuts. Pressing F2 or Ent er allows you to enter edit mode in the currently selected cell. To enter the same data in multiple cells, select the range and type the data, followed by Ctrl +Ent er. This action fills all selected cells with the same value.

Copying, cutting, and pasting Duplicate or moving data efficiently using keyboard short cuts. To copy the selected cells, press Ctrl+ C, and to cut the cells, use Ctrl+ X. To paste the copied or cut cells, press Ctr! +V. Additionally, Ctr! +D allows you to quickly fill in the data from the cell above, saving time when working with repetitive data.

Formatting Cells Formatting cells accurately and swiftly is crucial for data presentation. Use Ctr! +B, Ctr! +I, and Ctr! +U for bold, italic, and underlined formatting, respectively. Ctrl+ Shift +7 applies a strikethrough to the selected text, while Ctr! +S hift+5 ap p li es a strikethrough to the cell itself. Press Ctr! +1 to open the "Format Cells" dialog box and access various formatting options.

Working with Formulas and Functions:

Inserting Formulas To insert a formula into a cell, press the equals (=) key, followed by the formula expression. Use Tab to move to the next argument in the formula. Pressing Ctr! +Shift+ Enter applies an array formula, which allows calculations across multiple cells or ranges simultaneously.

AutoSum Function Accelerate your data analysis with the AutoSum function. After selecting a range of cells, press Alt+= (the equal sign) to instantly insert a SUM formula for the selected range. This shortcut saves time when performing common calculations.

Function

AutoComplete Reduce errors and save time when using functions by utilizing the Function AutoComplete feature. Begin typing the func-tion name and press Tab to see a list of matching functions. Select the desired function and continue typing, or press Enter to insert it into the cell.

Additional time-saving shortcuts

Undo and redo Cor rec t mistakes swiftly with the Undo and Redo shortcuts. Press Ctrl+ Z to undo your most recent action and Ctrl+ Y to redo it. These shortcuts help you maintain accuracy and easily revert changes.

Find and Replace Efficiently search for specific data in your spreadsheet using the Find and Replace shortcut s. Press Ctrl+ F to open the Find dialog box and Ctrl+ H to open the Replace dialog box. Enter the search or replacement term and navigate through the results using the Enter key.

USING ADD-ONS AND EXTENSIONS FOR ENHANCED FUNCTIONALITY
Installing and Managing Add-ons

Accessing the Add-on Market place The first step to expanding the functionality of Google Sheets is accessing the Add-ons Market place. From the menu, select "Add-ons" and then click on "Get add-ons." This will open the Add-ons Marketplace, where you can explore and in- stall various add-ons.

Installing Add-ons Browse through the available add-ons in the marketplace and select the ones that align with your needs. Click on the "Free" or "Purchase" button to install the desired add-on. Google Sheets will prompt you to grant the necessary permissions before in- stalling the add-on.

Managing Add-ons Once you have installed add-ons, you can manage them from the "Add-ons" menu. Use the "Man age add-ons" option to view all installed add-ons, disable or enable them, and access their respective settings.

Useful Add-ons for Google Sheets

Advanced Fin d and Replace The Advanced Find and Replace ad d-on offers powerful search and replace capabilities beyond the native functions of Google Sheets. It allows you to find and replace data based on specific criteria, such as using regular expressions or perform-ing case-sensitive searches. This add-on is especially valuable when working with large datasets or complex search patterns.

Power Tools Power Tools is a versatile add-on that provides a range of features to enhance data manipulation and analysis in Google Sheets. It includes tools for removing duplicates, splitting data into multiple columns, merging cells, generating random numbers, and much more. Power Tools simplifies common data tasks and saves you valuable time.

Mapping Sheets Mapping Sheets is an add-on that enables you to visualize data from your Google Sheets on interactive maps. You can plot addresses, postal codes, or geographic coordinates on a map and customize the appearance of markers and regions. This add-on is benefi-cial for data analysis, sales tracking, and presenting data in a visually appealing way.

Extensions for Google Sheets

Google Analytics: The Google Analytics extension provides direct access to your website's analytics data within Google Sheets. It allows you to import and analyze website metrics, such as pageviews, traffic sources, bounce rates, and conversion rates. With this extension, you can generate comprehensive reports and gain valuable insights into your website's performance. Save Emails and Attachments The Save Emails and Attachments extension simplifies the process of saving Gmail messages and their attachments directly to Google Sheets. You can create custom rules to automatically save specific emails or attachments based on criteria such as sender, subject, or label. This ex- tension is particularly useful for organizing and archiving important emails and their associated files.

Template Gallery by Vertex4 2 The Template Gallery extension provides a wide selection of pre-designed templates for various purposes, such as budgets, invoices, calendars, and project trackers. You can access and customize these templates directly from Google Sheets, sav- ing you time and effort when creating professional-looking documents.

Creating Custom Add-ons with Apps Script

Apps Script Overview Apps Script is a powerful development platform that allows you to create custom add-ons and extend the func-tionality of Google Sheets. With Apps Script, you can automate repetitive tasks, build custom functions, and create user interfaces within Google Sheets.

Creating Custom Add-ons By harnessing the capabilities of Apps Script, you can tailor Google Sheets to your specific needs. You can develop add-ons that automate data imports, perform complex calculations, generate reports, and more. The flexibility and customization offered by Apps Script empower you to create bespoke solutions that cater to your unique requirements.

Implementing Time-Saving Techniques and Best Practices

Organizing and Structuring Your Spreadsheet

Utilizing Tabs and Sheets Efficiently organize your data by utilizing tabs and sheets in Google Sheets. Create separate sheets for different categories or data sets within your spreadsheet. Use meaningful names for tabs and color-code them for easy identification. This organiza-tional structure makes it easier to locate and manage your data.

Grouping and Hiding Rows and Columns Grouping and hiding rows and columns is a handy technique to declutter your spreadsheet and focus on specific sections. Use the grouping feature to collapse or expand multiple rows or columns together, providing a cleaner view of your data. Additionally, hiding irrelevant rows or columns can help simplify complex spreadsheets and improve navigation.

Data Entry and Navigation Shortcuts:

AutoFill Accelerates data entry by utilizing the AutoFill feature in Google Sheets. Ent er a value or series of values in a cell, then drag the fill handle (a small square at the bottom right of the selected cell) to automatically populate adjacent cells with the same pattern. This saves time when entering repetitive data, such as dates, months, or numbered sequences.

Custom Lists Custom lists allow you to create predefined sequences or patterns for AutoFill. Define a custom list in the Google Sheets settings, such as a list of products or employee names, and then use it with AutoFill to quickly populate cells with the desired data. This technique ensures consistency and accuracy in data entry.

Go to Special The Go To Special feature is a powerful tool for navigating and selecting specific types of data in Google Sheets. Use this feature to quickly select all cells with formulas, constants, or conditional formatting. This helps in identifying and managing specific data elements within your spreadsheet.

Formulas and Function Optimization

Efficient Use of Formulas Optimize your formulas for improved performance and readability. Avoid excessive nesting of functions, as it can make formulas complex and difficult to trouble shoot. Instead, breakdown complex calculations into smaller, more manageable steps using helper columns or named ranges. This simplifies the formula structure and enhances its maintainability.

Array Formulas Array formulas are a powerful feature in Google Sheets that allow you to perform calculations on multiple cells or ranges simultaneously. By encapsulating the formula within an array formula syntax (using curly braces), you can eliminate the need for repeti-tive calculations and reduce the formula's size. This optimization technique improves calculation speed and efficiency.

Function Recalculation Control when and how often your functions recalculate to optimize performance. In large spreadsheets with complex formulas, you can set specific cells or ranges to recalculate manually or on a less frequent basis. This reduces unnecessary calcula-tions and speeds up the overall performance of your spreadsheet.

Collaboration and Sharing Best Practices

Sharing and Permissions When collaborating on Google Sheets, it's important to implement proper sharing and permissions settings. Only grant access to individuals who need it and assign appropriate levels of access (e.g., view, comment, or edit) to maintain data in-tegrity and privacy. Regularly review and update sharing permissions as needed.

Version History and Comments Take advantage of the version history feature to track changes made to your spreadsheet. This allows you to review and revert to previous versions if needed. Additionally, use comments to provide context, ask questions, or make suggestions within the spreadsheet. Comments foster effective communication and collaboration among team members.

Data Validation and Protection Implement data validation rules to ensure data integrity and consistency. Use data validation to restrict input options, set numeric ranges, or create dropdown menus within cells. Additionally, protect important data and formulas by applying for sheet and range protection. This prevents accidental modifications and safeguards critical information.

TROUBLESHOOTING COMMON ISSUES AND ERRORS

Google Sheets is a powerful tool for data management and analysis, but like any software, it can encounter issues and errors from time to time. When faced with these challenges, it is important to have troubleshooting skills to quickly identify and resolve problems. In this chapter, we will explore common issues and errors that users encounter in Google Sheets and provide practical solutions to overcome them.

Spreadsheet Performance Issues

Slow Loading or Response If your Google Sheets spreadsheet is slow to load or respond, several factors could be contributing to the issue. Firstly, check your internet connection to ensure it is stable. Addition ally, close any unnecessary browser tabs or applications that maybe consuming system resources. If the issue persists, try opening the spreadsheet in an incognito or private browsing window to rule out any conflicting browser extensions. If the problem continues, consider splitting the spreadsheet into smaller, more manageable sheets or opti-mizing formulas to improve performance.

Large File Size Large file sizes can impact the performance of Google Sheets. To reduce file size, remove any unnecessary data, such as empty rows or columns. Minimize the use of formatting, especially conditional formatting, as it can significantly increase file size. Addi-tionally, consider archiving older data or using external data sources, such as Google Drive or external databases, to store and reference large datasets without bloating the spreadsheet file size.

Formula and Calculation Errors

- **#REF! Errors** The #REF! error occurs when a formula references a cell or range that no longer exists or has been moved. To fix this error, review the formula and update the cell references accordingly. If the referenced cell or range was deleted, restore it or modify the formula to reference a valid cell or range.
- **#DIV/0! Errors** The #DIV/0! error appears when a formula attempts to divide a value by zero. To resolve this error, add an IF statement to check for a zero divis or before performing the division. For example, you can modify the formula to return a specific value or display a cus-tom error message when the divisor is zero.
- **NIA Errors** The #N/Aerror occurs when a formula cannot find the value it is looking for. This can happen when using functions like

VLOOKUP or I NDEX/ MATCH. Check the data being searched to ensure it is accurate and matches the criteria specified in the formula. If the data is not found, consider using the IFERROR function to display a custom message or handle the error gracefully.

Sharing and Collaboration Issues

Sharing Permissions and Access If you encounter issues with sharing and collaboration, ensure that the correct permissions have been granted to the intended collaborators.

Double-check the sharing settings and confirm that the individuals you want to share the spread- sheet with have the appropriate level of access (view, comment, or edit). If collaborators still cannot access the spreadsheet, check their email addresses for accuracy and resend the invitation if necessary.

Conflicting Edits and Version History When multiple users edit a spreadsheet simultaneously, conflicts can arise. Google Sheets automati-cally saves changes in real time, but conflicting edits may need to be resolved manually. If conflicts occur, a notification will appear, allow-ing you to review and choose which edits to keep. Addition ally, use the version history feature to revert to previous versions if needed.

Connectivity and Integration Issues

Int er net Connectivity If you are experiencing issues with connectivity, ensure that you have a stable internet connection. Check other websites or applications to confirm if the problem is specific to Google Sheets or if it extends to your entire network. If the issue persists, try using Google Sheets on a different device or network to determine if the problem is localized.

Add-ons and Extensions Add-ons and extensions can sometimes cause compatibility or performance issues in Google Sheets. If you encounter problems after installing an add-on or extension, disable or un install lit to see if the issue is resolved. Additionally, ensure that your add-ons and extensions are up to date, as outdated versions can cause conflicts.

CONCLUSION

As we reach the end of this journey into the world of digital spreadsheets, it's worth reflecting on the transformative power that tools like these can have in both our personal and professional lives. In many ways, working with spreadsheets is much more than simply entering data into cells; it's about understanding the potential that data holds, harnessing it, and using it to make informed decisions. Whether you started with no prior knowledge or had some experience under your belt, the path you've traveled is one of empowerment.

Learning to effectively use a tool that organizes, analyzes, and presents data in a way that's not only structured but also intuitive allows you to take control of information in ways you may not have considered before. Through this learning process, you've likely discovered that working with a digital spreadsheet tool isn't limited to one particular industry, profession, or task. Its versatility is one of its greatest strengths, and as you've seen, it can apply to everything from personal budgeting and project management to complex data analysis and collaboration with teams.

In today's data-driven world, the ability to organize and analyze information is a skill that pays dividends in multiple areas of life. Think about all the ways that spreadsheets can be used. They are essential for finance and accounting, helping businesses and individuals alike track income, expenses, and investments. They assist in project management, enabling the tracking of milestones, deadlines, and responsibilities. They also serve as invaluable tools for inventory management, customer data analysis, and sales tracking, allowing businesses to stay on top of their operations with precision.

However, beyond these conventional uses, spreadsheets also serve more creative and unexpected purposes. People use them to plan events, track workouts, and even manage their households. The possibilities are endless, and as you've seen throughout this book, the tools provided allow you to go far beyond simple calculations. Formulas, functions, automation, and data analysis features open up possibilities that may once have seemed out of reach.

The cloud-based nature of the tool we've explored also provides unique advantages that make it stand out among other spreadsheet platforms. The ability to work from anywhere, at any time, and collaborate seamlessly with others is invaluable in our increasingly connected world. Whether you're working from a coffee shop, sharing files with a global team, or simply updating a family budget from your smartphone, the accessibility of cloud-based spreadsheets has revolutionized how we think about productivity and collaboration.

In today's fast-paced environment, efficiency is key. Mastering the use of shortcuts and tools like this one can dramatically reduce the amount of time you spend managing your data. Think about the countless hours you can save by using formulas and functions to perform calculations, rather than doing them by hand. Consider the level of insight you can gain by creating dynamic charts and graphs that help you visualize data in meaningful ways, revealing patterns and trends that might otherwise go unnoticed. And imagine how much more productive you can be by automating repetitive tasks, freeing up your time to focus on higher-level analysis and decision-making.

Automation has undoubtedly been one of the highlights of this journey. For many people, the idea of automating tasks may have seemed intimidating or reserved for tech experts. But as you've learned, automation doesn't have to be complex. The tools available make it easy to record and implement macros, allowing you to streamline processes and create efficiencies that will save time and effort in the long run. It's a clear example of how technology is constantly evolving to make our lives easier, and how even a seemingly simple spreadsheet can serve as a powerful tool for automation and innovation.

Equally important is the collaborative aspect. In today's globalized world, the ability to collaborate in real time with people from all over the world is no longer a luxury—it's a necessity. Whether you're working with colleagues across departments or continents, the platform's real-time sharing, commenting, and editing features ensure that everyone stays on the same page. This level of collaboration enables seamless communication, reduces the risk of errors, and improves overall productivity. It's not just about creating and editing a spreadsheet; it's about working together to achieve a common goal.

Another crucial takeaway from this journey has been the focus on data management. It's easy to overlook the importance of keeping data organized, but as you've seen, managing data effectively is the key to unlocking its potential. It's not enough to simply gather information; you need to store it in a way that's logical, accessible, and easy to interpret. Tools like filtering, sorting, and formatting allow you to present data in a way that makes sense, ensuring that you—and anyone else who views your spreadsheet—can quickly find and understand the information that matters most.

Visualization is another important theme to reflect upon. Spreadsheets are not just about rows and columns of numbers. Through charts, graphs, and conditional formatting, you can transform raw data into something visually compelling and easy to understand. In doing so, you enhance your ability to communicate insights, whether you're presenting to a team of colleagues, pitching to investors, or simply organizing your thoughts for personal projects. These tools give you the power to convey complex information in a way that is both digestible and impactful.

And of course, no journey with spreadsheets would be complete without mentioning formulas and functions. The ability to perform complex calculations quickly and accurately is one of the fundamental reasons why people turn to spreadsheets in the first place. Whether you're using basic operations like addition and subtraction or diving into more advanced formulas, you've seen how formulas can help you analyze data in a way that goes beyond simple arithmetic. They allow you to draw insights, spot trends, and make predictions that can inform your decisions.

The road to mastering these tools is a continuous one. The more you use the platform, the more you'll discover its capabilities. New features are constantly being introduced, and as you continue to experiment and explore, you'll find ways to further optimize your workflows and achieve your goals. Every function you learn, every formula you master, adds to your skill set and enables you to work smarter, not harder.

The journey you've undertaken has prepared you to handle a wide range of tasks with confidence. You've learned how to navigate the interface, use keyboard shortcuts, perform basic and advanced calculations, format your spreadsheets, and collaborate with others. You've seen how to organize and manage your data effectively, and you've gained the skills to analyze that data and extract valuable insights. More importantly, you've learned how to take full advantage of the powerful tools that lie at the heart of modern spreadsheet software.

Ultimately, the skills you've developed through this process will continue to serve you long after you close this book. Whether you're using spreadsheets in your daily work, for personal projects, or in collaboration with others, you now have the knowledge and tools to approach any task with confidence and efficiency. The beauty of this platform is that it adapts to your needs, whether you're working on a simple budget or a complex data analysis project. Its versatility means that you can always find new ways to use it, regardless of your profession or area of interest.

As you move forward, continue to embrace the possibilities that this tool offers. Keep experimenting, keep learning, and most importantly, keep finding ways to make your work and your life more organized, efficient, and productive. The time and effort you've invested in mastering this tool will pay off in ways both big and small, helping you achieve your goals and stay ahead in an increasingly data-driven world.

In conclusion, mastering this tool has not only equipped you with a powerful skill set but also given you the confidence to tackle a wide range of tasks with ease. You now have the tools to manage data, analyze trends, collaborate effectively, and automate processes, all of which are essential skills in the modern world. As you continue to use these features, remember that the journey doesn't end here. There will always be more to learn, more ways to optimize your workflows, and more opportunities to use these skills to your advantage. Embrace this knowledge and continue to build on it, and you'll find that the possibilities are truly limitless.

Printed in Great Britain
by Amazon